A PASSION FOR FLYING

A Passion for Flying

8,000 Hours of RAF Flying

Group Captain Tom Eeles BA, FRAeS

Pen & Sword
AVIATION

First published in hardback format in 2008
and again in paperback format in 2015 by
PEN & SWORD AVIATION
An imprint of
Pen & Sword Books Ltd
47 Church Street
Barnsley, South Yorkshire
S70 2AS

ISBN 978 1 47384 564 0

A CIP catalogue record for this book is
available from the British Library.

Typeset in Palatino by
Phoenix Typesetting, Auldgirth, Dumfriesshire

Printed and bound in England
By CPI Group (UK) Ltd, Croydon, CR0 4YY

Pen & Sword Books Ltd incorporates the Imprints of Aviation, Atlas,
Family History, Fiction, Maritime, Military, Discovery, Politics, History,
Archaeology, Select, Wharncliffe Local History, Wharncliffe True Crime,
Military Classics, Wharncliffe Transport, Leo Cooper, The Praetorian Press,
Remember When, Seaforth Publishing and Frontline Publishing.

For a complete list of Pen & Sword titles please contact
PEN & SWORD BOOKS LIMITED
47 Church Street, Barnsley, South Yorkshire, S70 2AS, England
E-mail: enquiries@pen-and-sword.co.uk
Website: www.pen-and-sword.co.uk

Contents

Preface

Annual Confidential Reports are an unavoidable feature of life in the Services. Even after more than forty years in uniform I could not escape them. It was therefore with some pleasure that, during the ritual debrief of my final report, I heard from my squadron commander on Cambridge University Air Squadron that I still had 'a passion for flying after all these years'.

The phrase 'a passion for flying' stuck in my mind and so after finishing my time with the squadron in late 2004 I decided to record my experiences in the cockpit, over a period of more than forty years, before the passage of time dimmed my memories. It was a fascinating era to have been involved with the RAF. The RAF that I joined still had a permanent global presence and operated a huge variety of aircraft, despite the 1957 Sandys White Paper that indicated that there was no future for manned military aircraft. The Cold War was at its height and involved nearly every RAF unit in some way or other, yet we still had many major commitments in the Commonwealth. Our combat aircraft were primitive by today's standards, yet in terms of pure performance they were exciting and challenging to operate. Nuclear weapons featured significantly in our inventory; today the RAF has none.

I was lucky enough to be involved in a wide range of military flying activity, a large proportion being in the strike/attack business. But I also dabbled in air defence and had a long association with flying training in all its variety, ranging from operational conversion right down to elementary teaching. I avoided ground tours wherever possible and in this I had a high success rate. Even when trapped in an office I seemed able to escape back into the air at the slightest excuse.

As this wonderful experience now draws to a close I can look back and say that I always looked forward to going to work in the morning, apart perhaps when stuck on a ground tour. I hope you enjoy sharing my experiences in the air, some good, some not, some hilarious, some serious. My thanks go to my wife and family for their encouragement to set all this down 'for the record', and to my publishers, Pen and Sword, for their support.

Prologue

It was 4 January 1967. The Singaporean sun shone as bright as ever over the RAF Changi Fairy Point Officer's Club swimming pool, social centre and pride of the Headquarters Far East Air Force, yet somehow it didn't seem quite such an idyllic day like the last few had been. Various pilots and observers from 801 Naval Air Squadron lounged around the pool, eyeing up the female talent, but without the same enthusiasm that had been evident in the previous fortnight. Instead of the normal glasses of Tiger beer they were clutching innocuous drinks such as Coca-Cola or orange juice. The local Chinese barman was intrigued; what was it that had caused this unusual change in the pattern of their behaviour? Very soon the answer to this conundrum appeared, quite literally from around the corner of Changi creek. The great grey bulk of the aircraft carrier HMS *Victorious* came into view, steaming slowly down the narrow tidal waterway towards the open South China Sea. We watched her with critical eyes as she slowly slid past us. Today was the day that we were due to re-embark, and for me it would be my first time landing on board.

My goodness, she really doesn't look very big, was my immediate reaction. Up to now my visits to her had been confined to the Royal Navy dockyard in Singapore, where, lying alongside the quay, she had seemed really quite large, certainly large enough in which to become comprehensively lost whilst exploring inside her. My small number of worldly possessions was now buried down on 6 deck, in cabin 6Q6. It was really not much larger than a medium-sized wardrobe, with easy access to a large hole just outside the door giving a view of a rotating propeller shaft many feet below. This afternoon we were all going to re-embark after the Christmas and New Year break, spent by most of the Squadron's bachelors in the fleshpots of downtown Singapore.

There had been some flying during this period, which involved getting used to operating the Buccaneer in the steaming tropical heat and carrying out many sessions of MADDLS (Mirror Assisted Dummy Deck Landings), the nearest one could simulate carrier-landing techniques ashore. Not only did this annoy the permanent RAF residents of RAF Changi, who were all in the rather more sedate transport and maritime patrol business, but also a 200 feet wide, 9000-foot long runway that never moved, could never be like a small metal flight deck 700 feet long by 60 feet wide, 50 feet above the sea, with a habit of moving up and down and travelling around at 25 knots. The married men on the Squadron had now all returned from their leave in the UK, leaving behind their families. The Squadron was up to full strength, and as the Fleet Air Arm's first squadron to be embarked at sea with the S2 version of the Buccaneer, the eyes of the Royal Navy were on us. We downed our drinks, paid our bills, gathered up our few bits and pieces and made our way to the Naval Aircraft Support Unit where the Sea Vixens and Buccaneers were waiting on the hardstanding.

There then followed the inevitable delay associated with carrier operations whilst the ship found a suitable piece of sea to sail around in whilst recovering its Air Group. The Wessex helicopters and Gannet airborne early warning aircraft were the first to land on, followed by the Sea Vixen all-weather fighters. Finally, we were given our 'Charlie' time and launched out of Changi, with ever-increasing anticipation and, in my case, a degree of apprehension. By this time the usual afternoon tropical storms had brewed up, the sun had disappeared, the clouds had rolled in and the wind had picked up, kicking up a short steep sea in the piece of ocean where *Victorious* was sailing. As a consequence *Victorious* started to pitch gently as she sailed into the prevailing wind for our recovery, making the business of deck landing, challenging enough at the best of times, now even more so. We carried out the requisite number of touch-and-go landings, interspersed with many wave offs owing to poor approaches and a pitching deck, until finally each of us was told to put the hook down and land on. Just at this point a squall came through and the ship began to pitch close to the limits; we were waved off and as all aircraft reached diversion fuel at about

the same time everyone went back to Changi for the night. I felt
a mixture of relief (at least I had been told to put my hook down
after some pretty poor attempts at deck landings) and disappointment – the Buccaneers were the only ones who hadn't
got back on board.

The next day the storms had all evaporated, the sun shone
brightly and off we all went again early in the morning, without
having time to worry about what lay ahead. The sea was
smooth, the deck steady, the ship was not pushing out much
funnel smoke – the conditions were perfect. After two hook-up
touch-and-go landings, I was told by Flyco to put the hook
down. My next approach was good and steady, nicely on the
approach path (as indicated by the projector sight 'meat ball'),
on centre line and slightly faster than the calculated datum
speed to allow for the 'cliff edge' effect as you approached the
round down, which always knocked off two or three knots of
speed. As the wheels hit the deck there was a massive deceleration that completely caught me by surprise. During my
conversion training on the Buccaneer I had carried out an
arrested landing on the airfield at Lossiemouth after a hydraulic
failure but the deceleration then was nothing like this. I was
flung forward into the front of the cockpit, my straps just
preventing violent contact with the instrument coaming. I made
a mental note to tighten the straps as hard as possible in future.
As the aircraft came rapidly to a standstill the flight deck crew
rushed out in front of me, indicating to me to get the hook up,
fold the wings and taxi off the landing area of the flight deck as
quickly as possible to allow the wire to be reset for the next
aircraft in the landing pattern, which was not far behind. Hook
up with left hand, fold wings with right hand, left hand back on
throttles, engage nosewheel steering with left thumb and follow
flight deck crew's marshalling instructions implicitly. In the
brief beforehand we had been told that if they marshalled you
over the side it was their fault, not yours – not a comforting
thought. Eventually, after much awkward manoeuvring in a
confined space, the aircraft came to a halt in the area known as
Fly 1, at the bow of the carrier.

I breathed a huge sigh of relief, shut down the engines and
slowly unstrapped. At last I had made it on board. Opening the
canopy, I slowly climbed down the ladder and looked at
the scene before me. By now the aircraft recovery was complete

and the ship was turning out of wind. With about 1000 hours' of land-based 'normal' flying under my belt, I was used to experiencing a total lack of motion in the outside world after landing, parking and vacating one's aircraft. Now, however, as I looked up, the horizon was tilted over and moving past at a fair rate as the ship continued her turn. The sensation was so disorientating that I had to clutch hard on the aircraft's access ladder to stop myself from falling over.

The Buccaneer that I flew that day was XN 981, coded 234. Very many years later, whilst wandering around an air display at Duxford, I noticed that there was a cast metal Buccaneer model, made by Corgi, painted in the colours worn by our aircraft when embarked on HMS *Victorious*. Naturally I had to buy it. When I got it home and unwrapped it, I discovered to my delight that it was XN 981. Further research in my logbook also revealed that XN 981 was also the aircraft in which I did my last catapult launch. What an extraordinary coincidence.

CHAPTER ONE

Prelude to Flying
– 1942 to 1960

I was born in September 1942 into an Air Force family. My father was one of the early Flight Cadets at Cranwell. He had a distinguished career in the RAF and was undoubtedly a strong influence on my life from an early stage. My memories of those early years are scant. I can remember being pushed into a cupboard under the stairs, presumably during a V1 attack. This must have been in 1944 when we were living at Stanmore as my father was at HQ Fighter Command. I also remember being terrified by Meteor aircraft attempting to gain the World Air Speed Record in 1946, when we lived for a while at Bognor Regis. They roared along the beach at low level and high speed – and I did not like this. Thus early omens for a flying career were not good. In late 1946 the family joined my father in the USA, where he was working as a member of the UK military delegation to the newly formed UN. Again, I remember little of our time in the USA, apart from swearing allegiance to the Stars and Stripes at the nursery school I attended and the chimney catching fire on Christmas Eve, when some surplus decorations were burnt. I was particularly concerned as to how this would affect Father Christmas's visit.

In 1948 we returned from the USA and my father was posted as Station Commander, RAF Thorney Island, a fighter base on the south coast near Chichester. By now my fear of noisy jet aircraft seems to have disappeared, as I have only the pleasantest of memories of our time here. Thorney Island in the summer of 1949 was a wonderful place for a small boy to live. It was home to three Meteor Mk 4 squadrons of Fighter Command. Additionally, there was the sea and acres of mud just yards away from the house we lived in. It was indeed a paradise. The constant comings and goings of the Meteors excited me enormously and first generated within me a wish to fly. On the Battle of Britain 'At Home' Day that summer I got airborne for the first time. It was in a somewhat decrepit de Havilland Dragon Rapide that was offering fifteen-minute joy rides at £1 a time and I persuaded my parents to let me have a go. I don't remember much about the flight but I'm sure I enjoyed it and perhaps thoughts of being an engine driver when I grew up must have begun to dim. Messing about in boats was another favourite occupation. Thorney Creek was full of boats of various sorts and I had an old surplus RAF single-seat dinghy of wartime vintage, which even had a mast and sail but was only capable of slow progress downwind. Thus the two seeds of the subsequent work and leisure activities throughout my life were planted.

We left Thorney Island in the summer of 1950 and off I went to a prep school in Sussex. After two fairly short appointments at RAF Old Sarum and SHAPE (Supreme Headquarters Allied Powers Europe) in Paris my father was appointed Commandant of the RAF College, Cranwell. You cannot imagine what delight this gave me, as my interest and desire to fly had been growing all the time at prep school. Living at Cranwell in the early 1950s merely made my wish to fly even greater. During the holidays there were Prentices, Harvards, Chipmunks, Balliols, Provosts, Ansons and the occasional Meteor and Vampire all to be seen and envied. There were very few opportunities to fly, but I do recall the occasional passenger trip in an Anson or Devon, probably quite illegal but the rules and regulations were only lightly applied in those days.

One summer term my uncle, Squadron Leader Bobby Eeles RAux AF, OC 615 Squadron, was detailed off to take me out of school for the day. It being a Sunday he collected me and took me off to RAF Biggin Hill, where his squadron was based. It was a glorious hot summer day and I was put down in front of the squadron offices in a deck chair, given a pile of Wagon Wheel biscuits to eat and told not to move. It was a busy day and there was a lot of flying going on. I decided to try and persuade Uncle Bobby to let me go up in a Meteor. Amazingly, he agreed. Still clad in my school blazer and shorts – there was no flying suit small enough – I was strapped into a parachute that I had little hope of using. I was strapped into the rear seat of a Meteor T7 on top of a large cushion so that I could see out.The pilot on this occasion was a gentleman called Mike D'Arcy – I forget his rank. He asked me what I would like to do. I replied – somewhat boldly – that I would like to go and beat up my school. As he did not know where it was I would have to get him there. This wasn't too difficult, all you had to do was follow the main road out of Tunbridge Wells for a few miles and there you were. The school was beaten up in fine Auxiliary Air Force style so we then went off to do some aerobatics. Much to Mike D'Arcy's disappointment I was not sick, the Wagon Wheels stayed down. After landing back at Biggin Hill, I knew for certain that military flying was the thing for me. Such an escapade would of course be impossible today, indeed I suspect Uncle Bobby went well beyond the boundaries of legality even for those days. I am eternally grateful to him and Mike D'Arcy for convincing me in no uncertain manner of what I wanted to do when I grew up.

In 1956 I moved to Sherborne School and my father was posted from Cranwell to the Air Ministry. School life became more serious with proper exams to pass and there were no more holidays to be spent on busy RAF Stations. However, the compensation was that there was a very active Combined Cadet Force at Sherborne. After the first year, which had to be spent in the Army Section, I moved across to the RAF Section in 1958 and for the first time put on an RAF uniform. Life in the RAF Section was fairly relaxed. We had a Grasshopper glider, but its use was banned because the only time it had been launched on the hallowed playing fields it had carved a huge groove across a rugby pitch on landing. Consequently the master in charge of the sports pitches refused permission for any further attempts at flight. However, we were very lucky in that our closest RAF Station was RAF Boscombe Down, the Aircraft and Armament Experimental Establishment, where our liaison officer was a pilot on the heavy aircraft test squadron. Many expeditions were made to Boscombe Down to fly around Wiltshire in the cavernous Beverley transport aircraft at a very pedestrian pace. I also recall short trips in the Harvard photo chase aircraft and in a Meteor T7.

The highlight for me occurred on my last visit, in the summer of 1960. By now a Sergeant in the RAF Section, I was lucky enough to be offered, on a field day visit, a trip in a Hunter T7. Again, it was a beautiful English summer's day as we took off and climbed to 40,000 feet over the Channel, this time considerably more legally than my first ever jet sortie with 615 Squadron five years before. After breaking the sound barrier I blacked out completely on the recovery from the dive, but the experience was unforgettable.

That summer we went for our camp to RAF Laarbruch, in Germany, a major base with Canberras and Javelin fighters. Plenty of flying was available in the Station Flight Chipmunk and I remember well a long night sortie in a Canberra B(I)8 of 16 Squadron; I sat on the rumble seat below the pilot and next to the navigator, virtually unable to see anything. Little did I realise at the time that only a few years later I would be doing the same thing on this squadron, but from the pilot's seat.

By now I had had an RAF Scholarship for two years and a guaranteed place at Cranwell provided I passed my dreaded A levels to the required standard. We were spending a summer holiday in a family farmhouse in Teesdale and I remember well going down to Richmond to the post office to get the telegram giving the results. I had passed. My last few days as a civilian passed very quickly. On 3 September 1960, I found myself with a large number of similar individuals on King's Cross station, waiting for the train to take us to Sleaford and then on to Cranwell to join the RAF.

CHAPTER TWO

Early Days – 1960 to 1963

The RAF College, Cranwell, was a demanding establishment in the early 1960s. During the first term we members of the Junior Entry were the lowest form of life. We lived in the South Brick Lines, a collection of ancient huts dating from World War One. Living in each hut were four of us new arrivals and a 'mentor' from the Entry above us to sort us out and show us the ropes. The hut had three rooms, a communal ablution area (the first room on entry), then a dormitory (heated by an ancient front-loading coke burning stove), then finally a study room with five desks. Everything had to be kept spotlessly clean. We slid around on the ancient lino floors to keep them scratch-free and shiny. No dust was permitted anywhere, beds had always to be immaculately made and all clothes had to be folded to an exact pattern and stored precisely in accordance with a diagram – no variation was permitted. Our lives were a continuous round of early morning starts, drill, kit inspections, more drill, very short haircuts, bulling boots, lectures on service discipline and similar subjects.

The slightest misdemeanour would result in one being placed on a charge, found inevitably guilty and being put on restrictions. Being on restrictions involved parading before life started in the morning in immaculate uniform, then joining the normal working day, then parading again at 1800 hrs in immaculate uniform. After this a period of strenuous drill took place, which resulted in a completely messed up uniform. There was then another inspection at 2200 hrs at which perfection was the only acceptable appearance. Any speck of dust or poorly blancoed webbing at any of these three parades resulted in yet more days on restrictions. It was a tough regime and some did not last through the first term.

Aircraft and flying did not feature and were not even thought about much with the pressure of surviving. We all dreaded 'Crowing', a form of ritual humiliation whereby members of the Senior Entry would swoop down on a luckless hut in the evening, when its inmates were busy cleaning, polishing or studying. The inmates were then required to perform a ridiculous task, such as mimicking the action of a four-stroke engine, or hanging upside down from the beams singing a song. Thankfully we did not suffer a great deal from this torture as it was being actively discouraged by the staff.

We were allowed out on a Saturday evening about halfway through the first term. We were not permitted to keep cars during the first term so we all took the bus into Lincoln, looking totally conspicuous with our minimalist haircuts, sports jackets, slacks and highly polished shoes. We could not have got up to much as we all had to be back in the hut by midnight! The nearer town of Sleaford was off limits to Flight Cadets, being reserved for the airmen.

It was always cold and great skill was needed to keep the coke stove on overnight without creating dust and mess. One hut foolishly decided to have the stove going the night before a particularly rigorous inspection was due to take place. After its inhabitants had bulled the interior to a gleaming state and had retired to bed, the inhabitants of the next-door hut climbed on to the roof and dropped a large firework down the chimney. The subsequent violent explosion blew the doors off the stove and filled the interior of the hut with a huge quantity of hot ash and red hot coals. Needless to say, despite working all night, they did not pass the inspection and ended up on restrictions, along with the next-door hut who were charged with destroying the stove, but not for too long as someone in authority saw the funny side of it.

We were looked after by our 'mentors' – mine was Alastair Campbell, a man of infinite patience and charm with whom I subsequently worked closely many years later. We were also driven hard by the fearsome drill sergeants, who turned us from an ill-disciplined rabble into a passably efficient bunch of Flight Cadets by the end of this first term.

The quality of life improved considerably in the second term, as there was another Junior Entry to take our place in the South Brick Lines. We moved to the much more comfortable barrack blocks flanking the Junior Entry parade square, which had single-room accommodation. Needless to say, these rooms had to be inspected regularly, but they had central heating and were much easier to keep clean.

We were now allowed to fly once a week in the Chipmunks, which operated from the North Airfield, a huge expanse of grass that we all had to run around once a year to compete for the Knocker Cup. I note that my first flight was with a Fg Off Nichols, in Chipmunk WB 550, on 25 January 1961. Most of this flying was done in the rear seat with a non-QFI (non-Qualified Flying Instructor) in the front and counted only as air experience. Occasionally one was lucky enough to get a QFI, which enabled proper dual instruction to be given; in the spring term of 1961 I got 2 hours 20 minutes' dual.

The Chipmunk was a classic design, simple to fly but difficult to fly well. It could bite back if you took liberties with it, especially when handling on the ground. On the ground the view from the front seat, normally the student's, was poor. It was even worse from the back seat. The engine was equipped with a cartridge starter that used cartridges similar to a 12-bore shotgun cartridge. After strapping in and checking the cockpit, you placed your hands outside the cockpit in view of the ground crew and called out 'Fuel on, brakes on, throttle closed, switches safe.' The ground crew would then open the engine cowling, insert the cartridge breech, tickle the carburettor to get fuel through, close the cowling and indicate it was clear to start by saying 'Breech inserted, cowling secure, rear switches on, clear to start.' You then pulled the starter cord, which fired the cartridge. There was a loud bang and with luck the engine would rotate, fire up and start running. If it failed to start you repeated the whole process again.

Taxiing the Chipmunk could be quite challenging. The brakes were controlled by a long lever that stuck up out of the cockpit floor on the left-hand side. If this lever was pulled fully rearwards and locked in position the brakes would be fully applied.

To obtain differential braking the lever was moved a small distance rearwards and locked; application of rudder then applied brake in the same direction, enabling the pilot to steer left or right. The aircraft also had a strong tendency to weather-cock into wind and the control column had to be used appropriately to keep the tail on the ground during taxiing. It was essential to weave continuously whilst taxiing to keep a clear view ahead. Thus a long taxi across the relative wind was a demanding exercise in co-ordination of hands, feet and eyes; safe arrival at the marshalling point was greeted with a sigh of relief.

Once in the air the Chipmunk flew beautifully. It was not a high-performance machine; it took a long time to climb to height and once up there would cruise happily at 90 knots. It had a standard instrument panel with the normal six instruments; the artificial horizon and the direction indicator were air driven so could topple very easily during manoeuvres. The fuel gauges were in the wing upper surface, connected directly to their tanks and rather awkward to read in flight. The flaps were controlled by a large lever on the right-hand side of the cockpit rather similar to a car's hand brake; you had to change hands on the control column to operate them, which could make a final approach interesting.

Stalling and spinning were completely viceless. Aerobatics were a delight but you would lose height steadily during an aerobatic sequence. You could not sustain negative g because of the carburettor fuel feed to the engine, which would cut out if you tried to sustain inverted flight, so slow rolls were challenging. Equally, the engine often stopped during stall turns but always got going again as you accelerated down after the manoeuvre. You had to be careful not to exceed the maximum permitted engine RPM (2675) when accelerating to high speed (a relative concept!) as the propeller was fixed pitch. The maximum permitted speed was 173 knots.

The circuit and landing procedure was straightforward, apart from the change-hands routine to lower the flaps. It was desir-able to land in a three-point attitude and the aircraft would bounce or ground loop if you got this wrong. The threshold speeds were very low: 55 knots for a normal approach, 60 knots flapless and 45 knots for a short landing. It was easier to land on grass surfaces than hard runways.

You could always imagine that you were in a World War Two fighter when flying the Chipmunk, but without the associated complexities and handling challenges. In sum, it was a lovely aircraft in which to achieve your first solo. In spite of the terrible smell of vomit in these Chipmunks – most had been used to provide air experience for ATC (Air Training Corps) cadets at some time – the flying made a welcome break from drill and academic studies.

By now academic studies for me meant being a member of the C stream, which involved study for an external degree with the University of London in history, english and war studies. I found war studies and history interesting but english was something of a trial.

At the end of the second term the Leadership (to us Survival) Camp took place. It was held in the wilds of the Scottish Highlands, miles from anywhere, near the source of the River Spey. It involved endless forced marches across the mountains, by day and night, being chased by members of the RAF Regiment, sleeping under canvas and outside, and eating very little. The journey from Grantham station to Newtonmore was an epic in itself, British Rail still being firmly in the steam train era. One or two were re-coursed after this episode. On the way home afterwards I fell asleep at the wheel of my ancient MG saloon and luckily slid gently off the road in Stockbridge, destroying the car and a wall but I suffered no injuries. I had only paid £20 for the car, so it wasn't a great loss.

Back at Cranwell for the summer and autumn terms, life continued much as before, with the improvement in quality of life in the autumn associated with the move from the Junior Entry's Mess up to main the College building. After some 6 hours 10 minutes' dual in the Chipmunk, spread over nearly a year, Master Pilot Ayers was bold enough to send me off solo on 16 October 1961, from Cranwell's North Airfield. That was the end of my Chipmunk flying at Cranwell and I didn't fly a Chipmunk again for twenty-seven years!

In January 1962 proper flying training started on the Jet Provost (JP), which was in service in two versions, the Mk 3 and the Mk 4. The Mk 4 had a considerably more powerful engine and was considered to be quite a hot ship. We spent half a day down at the flying squadrons learning to fly and half a day on academic or Service studies. Learning to fly and studying a degree course at the same time, as well as surviving as a Flight Cadet, proved to be quite a challenge. There were many times when I felt I had only survived by the skin of my teeth.

I went solo after 9 hours 55 minutes' dual, on 2 February 1962, in Jet Provost Mk 3 fleet number 56. And thereby hangs a tale. Thirty-one years later, when I was Station Commander at RAF Linton on Ouse, the Jet Provost was finally being retired after many years of excellent service. In one of my weekly executive meetings I asked the engineering contract manager, Terry Stone, if it would be possible to retain a Jet Provost as a Gate Guardian for the Station. He confirmed that this was indeed possible so I asked him to pick a suitable airframe that had not already been disposed of, preferably a Mk 3 as this version had been in service the longest. Eventually the selected aircraft was ready for positioning on display and Terry produced a plaque, which detailed the aircraft's service history. I observed that I could well have flown this aircraft as it had been at Cranwell whilst I was there, but that as I had only recorded fleet numbers in my logbook it would be impossible to tell. Terry offered to look through the F700 to see if he could find my signature; I told him not to bother. He then asked to see my logbook. He then announced in triumph that it was the Jet Provost that I had flown my first (jet) solo in – the dates coincided precisely in both the logbook and F700. So finally I knew the aircraft's proper identity – XN 589, now fleet number 46 at Linton. The faithful JP is still there to this day.

The JP was a jet-powered version of the Piston Provost, powered by a Viper turbojet and equipped with retractable landing gear. The Viper had originally been developed as a 'throw away' engine for the Jindivik target drone but had been adapted for normal use in the JP. The JP had side-by-side seating, ejection seats, a UHF radio and a simple DME navigation aid. It represented quite an advance in sophistication when compared with the Piston Provost but the Mk 3 was very underpowered. It was easy to start and taxi with its nosewheel landing gear. The take-off and climb was unexciting, the normal cruising speed was 180 knots and we tended to operate in the height band of 5000 feet to 20,000 feet. It was fully aerobatic and capable of more advanced manoeuvres than the simple Chipmunk, such as 'noddy' stall turns, proper slow rolls, four- and eight-point rolls, reverse stall turns and sustained inverted flight. It was straight-forward to fly in the landing circuit as long as you remembered to raise and lower the landing gear every time around. It was equipped with a fairly good instrument layout with an electri-cally driven artificial horizon and a gyro magnetic compass. The instruments were grouped in the centre of a fairly wide instru-ment panel, which meant that you had to look across the cockpit at them from your seat on the left-hand side but you soon got used to this. The Mk 4 version had an uprated Viper engine so was always in demand for aerobatics. It had a much more exciting performance, being capable of achieving speeds of 400 knots and altitudes around 30,000 feet. Neither version was pressurised and they both had the same rather primitive oxygen system, which did not supply oxygen under pressure. During high-level handling sorties in the Mk 4 we were regularly exposed to conditions favourable for decompression sickness and most of us experienced this in some form or other.

The flying syllabus was 180 hours, an extra 20 hours being added to the Cranwell syllabus to compensate for the extra time spent in training by Cranwell cadets compared with our direct-entry colleagues. The syllabus followed a traditional pattern. After an initial spell of general handling we were soon intro-duced to the circuit and expected to go solo between 10 to 15 hours. Some went sooner, some later. We were then introduced to more off-circuit general handling and aerobatics, with an initial progress check after about 30 hours. Spinning was carried out both dual and solo, the only limitation being that spinning was prohibited with fuel in the tip tanks. Instrument flying followed, with award of an instrument flying grading, a very lowly form of instrument rating that allowed a student to penetrate cloud in a straight line. Medium- and low-level navi-gation, night flying and formation flying all featured in the syllabus, including land-away cross-country navigation exercises.

For the next eighteen months we alternated between flying and academics during term time, progressing steadily through the syllabus. It was a great relief to spend time down on the flying squadron, away from the fierce Senior NCOs and Flight Commanders up at the College. Inevitably one or two got the chop from flying; some stayed on as navigators or ground branch, some left for another life. Occasionally there was an accident but these were few and far between and never affected us much.

Lincolnshire had a number of Thor ballistic missile sites, manned and operated by the RAF, which were excellent landmarks for us tyro aviators. I remember well how surprised we were to see all these sites with their full complements of missiles all up and ready during the tense time of the Cuban Missile Crisis, whilst we carried on doing aerobatics overhead them in the autumn of 1962.

The winter of 1962/3 was very severe and had a big effect on our flying activities. There was snow on the ground from December until March and large amounts of it fell in Lincolnshire. There was no snow-clearing equipment at Cranwell, other than cadets wielding shovels and brushes and the occasional snowplough. The airfield at Cranwell was covered with a deep layer of snow, so Wing Commander Flying decided that Barkston Heath seemed a better option for clearing the snow; the entire Cadet Wing was given shovels and set to work clearing the runway. Progress was very slow and at the end of the first day one of the mathematicians amongst us calculated that at this rate of progress it would take until May to clear the runway. Thankfully, this exercise was soon discontinued. Some of the JPs were then dragged out onto Cranwell's snow-covered runway and launched off, sliding about quite dangerously, to land at Coningsby, where there was snow-clearing equipment.

Coningsby was a Vulcan base, which had to be kept open all the time so that the British nuclear deterrent force could be seen to be operational. We then went by bus to Coningsby to fly for quite a while. Strenuous efforts were made by the Squadron Commanders at Coningsby to interest us in the Vulcan force; one look inside a Vulcan convinced me that they were to be avoided at all costs in the future. A final treat at the very end of the flying course was a weekend trip to RAF Wildenrath in Germany, when three aircraft went out on a Friday and returned the next Monday.

*   *   *

Ancient cars featured strongly in our lives at Cranwell. The Cadets' garage was a decrepit hangar dating from World War One, draughty and without lighting. Rows of cars in varying states of disrepair clustered inside; every Saturday afternoon there was a flurry of activity by their owners attempting to get them into running order for the evening foray into Lincoln, or, for the very brave and confident, Nottingham. There was no MOT test in those days. The variety of types was amazing, including an ancient Lagonda saloon that had had its body removed and replaced by a Vampire T11's nose cone, thereby making it into a giant two-seater sports car – without a hood. I owned no fewer than five cars during my three years at Cranwell – one lasted only three weeks! My favourite, and the longest lasting, was 'Bessie', a 1931 Morris Cowley. She was bright yellow, an open two-seater with a dickey seat at the back. Her maximum speed under favourable conditions was 40 mph. She was the most reliable of the five and I sold her for £30 at the end of my time at Cranwell as I doubted she would ever make it to RAF Valley. Today, if she existed, she would be worth a small fortune.

The first ever RAF Regiment Cadet was involved in a car-stealing ring – without anyone's knowledge. The Cadets' garage provided a perfect cover for his nefarious activities – Cadets changed cars almost weekly and no one took any notice of his acquisitions and disposals. He was caught out when he put one of his many current tax discs on his car of the day, which unfortunately belonged to another – stolen – car. He took it to London for the weekend and parked it illegally; it was spotted by a policeman who noted the discrepancy and one evening he was taken away to jail by two plain-clothes policemen. This was sensational and definitely one in the eye for the RAF Regiment staff who were constantly singing his praises. When the MOT test was introduced in 1963 it swept through the Cadets' garage like the Black Death and many wonderful old cars were destined never to be driven again.

Finally, it all came to an end. After sitting exams for the University of London and obtaining a low-quality pass – third class-degree in History, English and War Studies – I managed to pass the Final Handling Test, flown on 1 July with a Sqn Ldr Foster. Then there was the longed-for logbook entry authorising the wearing of the Royal Air Force flying badge with effect from 30 July 1963, in accordance with Queen's Regulation 770, after 116 hours' dual and 65 hours' solo. Air Chief Marshal Sir Gus Walker, the C-in-C of Flying Training Command, presented us with our 'Wings' that evening. Next morning we all paraded for the last time as Flight Cadets with Wings on our tunics. We marched up the College steps to the tune of 'Auld Lang Syne' and raced to our rooms to put on our Pilot Officer uniforms. We woke the next morning with hangovers after the Passing Out Ball and moved on into the real Air Force.

CHAPTER THREE

Advanced Flying Training and Operational Conversion – 1963 to 1964

The next stop was No. 4 Flying Training School, RAF Valley, Anglesey, where we were to do our advanced flying training on the Gnat T1. The Gnat T1 was brand new and was still rolling off the production line. The Gnat was built by the Folland Aircraft Company and was designed by W E Petter, who had also designed the Canberra, the Lightning, and also the Westland Whirlwind twin-engined cannon armed fighter, which my father had helped bring into service in 1940. Originally the Gnat was conceived as a small lightweight fighter in an attempt to halt the trend towards ever bigger and heavier fighter aircraft. As such it was ordered by the Finnish Air Force in small numbers and large numbers were built under licence in India, but did not find favour with the RAF. In the early 1960s the RAF needed a new advanced trainer to replace the ageing Vampire T11, which was not considered a suitable lead in for the new generation of combat aircraft coming into service. The Hunter T7 was available but an argument was put forward by Folland's designers that the Hunter could not embody the new Integrated Flight Instrument System known as OR 946, whereas the trainer version of the Gnat that the firm was proposing would be able to incorporate OR 946, albeit in a modified form. Also, just at the same time the Hunter had beaten the Gnat in the competition to provide a replacement ground attack fighter for the Venom, so almost as a consolation prize the Gnat T1 was ordered to replace the Vampire.

The Gnat was a very small aircraft, only 37 feet long and with a wing span of 24 feet. The student and instructor sat one behind the other and the rear cockpit layout was quite different from the front (student's) cockpit because of the small size of the aircraft. The landing gear also doubled as an airbrake (when partially extended) and retracted into the fuselage, having a very narrow track of only 5 feet. Retracting the landing gear resulted in a major rearward movement of the centre of gravity and an automatic tailplane datum shift was incorporated to compensate for this.

The flying controls were hydraulically operated but there was a manual reversion facility in the event of a hydraulic failure. This could be practised in flight by selecting a hydraulic cock 'off', which cut off hydraulic pressure from the flying controls. Sneaky instructors would turn this off at most inconvenient moments, such as in the middle of your aerobatic sequence. Following a simulated or real hydraulic failure it was essential to 'freeze' the tailplane in the right position, as control in pitch was now provided by very small elevators, which were unlocked from the tailplane by pulling a T-shaped handle in the cockpit. The elevators were so small that they could not provide sufficient control authority for safe flight and landing, so the 'frozen' tail could be moved in the nose-up sense by use of a standby electrical trim system. It could only be moved back to the original frozen position. In manual the datum shift facility did not work so had to be compensated for by the pilot. Control loads in manual were much heavier than in power, so handling following a hydraulic failure could be very challenging, especially if associated with an engine failure as the forced landing pattern was more difficult to fly than the simple Jet Provost's.

The emergency drill following a hydraulic failure, real or simulated, is burnt into every Gnat pilot's brain. Its acronym was STUPRECC. This translated as: 'Speed – below 400 knots/0.85 M, Trim – to ideal sector while regaining level flight, Unlock – elevators, Power – cock off, Raise – guard on standby trim, Exhaust – tailplane and aileron accumulators, Check – operation of elevators, ailerons and standby trim, Changeover – switches to standby if required.' It was a complicated drill and if you got it wrong there was a good chance of losing control at a critical moment, such as just before touchdown.

The Gnat was powered by an Orpheus turbojet; this was started by an external gas turbine starter trolley, which was almost as big as the aircraft. Landing away at an airfield that did not have these starters was embarrassing! With its very narrow track landing gear the Gnat could be very tricky in cross winds and had a limit of 10 knots crosswind on a wet runway. A brake parachute was also fitted but it was quite small and not very effective. Compared with the rather pedestrian Jet Provost it was a really hot ship, capable of exceeding its maximum IAS (indicated airspeed) limit of 0.9 M below 11,000 feet and 500 knots above. Supersonic flight was easy to achieve from a shallow dive, normally entered from around 40,000 feet. It only carried 2120 lb of fuel internally and so for flying training always had external slipper tanks fitted, which increased fuel capacity to 3063 lb – just enough for an hour's sortie. The Orpheus turbojet delivered 4520 lb static thrust at sea level. It was a reliable engine and we very rarely suffered from malfunctions, despite the salt-laden corrosive environment in which it operated.

Unlike other RAF aircraft the Gnat was not fitted with Martin-Baker ejection seats. Instead, it had lightweight seats made by Folland to an original design by SAAB of Sweden. Their operation was quite different to the Martin-Baker seats; they were much lighter and slimmer, yet they worked very well. Instead of a collection of safety pins, which had to be removed to make the seat live (the Martin-Baker system), there was a simple lever with a large red knob on the end that was in line with the pilot's neck in the safe position, which was moved 90 degrees to the right to make the seat live. It was very simple and effective. If you tried to get airborne with the seat safe, the acceleration on take-off pressed your neck firmly into the red knob, reminding you forcibly to make the seat live!

The OR 946 flight instrument system was a great advance over the traditional instruments in the JP and made instrument flying much easier than in the JP. The view from the front seat was excellent and you could imagine you were riding a witch's broomstick when looking out ahead at the very long pitot probe.

We were the second course to fly the Gnat, so the overall level of knowledge and experience of the aircraft was still fairly low amongst the staff. The general serviceability of the Gnat was not good; it was a very complex aircraft and because of its small size and compact nature, any engineering problems were always difficult to resolve. During its service the Gnat was to suffer from a high loss rate, mainly caused by handling difficulties associated with the longitudinal control system and the general complexity of its systems. Nevertheless, it was very exhilarating to fly. Your first solo was a circuit of Anglesey as fast as possible, which was fantastic fun. The course was some 70 hours long and I found it much more challenging than basic flying training. The syllabus covered the same activities as the basic JP course – general handling, instrument flying, night flying, formation and navigation – with the added sophistication of a flight simulator in which countless complicated emergency drills were practised.

RAF Valley was a remote and bleak place to be based, especially in the autumn and winter. The airfield buildings all dated from the 1940s and were primitive. The Officers' Mess was somewhat newer and a big building programme was being undertaken to upgrade the Station. The grim prospect of a posting to V bombers at the end of the course was ever present as output from RAF Valley went in that direction in those days, particularly if you did not do very well. The incentive to perform to a high standard was therefore very strong. Social life was confined to Anglesey with the occasional epic weekend drives to London. There were few motorways then and the M1 stopped at Birmingham, so a car journey to London was not undertaken lightly. On Sundays no pubs were open in that part of Wales, although there were some dubious 'clubs' where a drink could be found, and the Officers' Mess bar always did a roaring trade.

The senior course (consisting entirely of the Cranwell Entry ahead of ours) decided one day to steal a guided missile which was displayed on a stand outside the Officers' Mess at the neighbouring Army firing range of Ty Croes. They reckoned that they could fit it into the back of a long wheelbase Land Rover, which they borrowed from a local farmer. Equipped with hacksaws and candles to deaden the noise of sawing they bluffed their way in successfully. They had arranged with one of the building contractors to have a supply of ready-mix concrete and a suitable hole waiting back on the lawn in front of the bar at RAF Valley so that their trophy could be secured in its new home for all to see. Unfortunately, the metal stand holding up the missile proved to be solid, not hollow as they had expected, so sawing through it took very much longer than they had calculated. Amazingly, no one detected them whilst they struggled on. Eventually they got the missile off its stand only to discover it was very heavy and far too long to go in the back of the Land Rover. Nothing daunted, they propped it up on the back of the Land Rover, pointing forward like something on a May Day Parade in Red Square, and succeeded in driving out of the camp without being stopped at the Guardroom! The hole and concrete were ready back at RAF Valley but sadly the missile arrived much later than had been expected.

It was placed in position and when we all awoke in the morning there it was, looking splendid. Naturally, at first light the Army realised their loss and where their rocket had gone – there was no other possible place apart from RAF Valley. They turned up very quickly demanding the return of their property, and despite offers of trips in Gnats and tours of the Station, they removed the missile before the concrete had had time to set, but luckily after photographs had been taken. By way of revenge the Army removed a large wooden propeller from the ante-room wall. As few of us used the ante-room, preferring the bar for socialising, no one noticed it had gone and the Army had to ring up to ask if we wanted it back!

By February 1964 our course had come to an end (not with the same number who had started) and it was time to find out one's posting to the front line. There were the usual lucky few who went to Hunters, three even luckier chaps went off to be the first ab initio Lightning pilots and one or two went to Central Flying School (CFS) to become first tour QFIs. I was lucky, too, as I escaped the V force and was the only one on the course to be posted to Canberras. I was quite happy with this fate – I certainly had not performed well enough to go on to single-seat aircraft and all Canberra squadrons were now based overseas and operated, by and large, at low level. They were all single-pilot aircraft so I was entirely content with my lot.

*   *   *

There then followed a delightful interlude whilst I awaited a course on the Canberra Operational Conversion Unit. I went as a holding officer to RAF Colerne, just outside Bath, to be attached to a Hastings transport squadron. The Hastings was a lumbering, four-engine tail dragger, which owed its origins to the Handley Page Halifax heavy bomber of the World War Two era. I was told that the only reason it had been equipped with a tailwheel rather than a nosewheel was to enable an Army jeep to be slung under the wing centre section! The wings and engines were I believe identical to the Halifax's. The Hastings was the RAF's main medium-sized tactical freight and troop transport aircraft and despite its antiquated appearance it did an excellent job. It was robust and simple, but tricky to take off and land. It was replaced in service in 1968 by the Hercules but a few soldiered on well into the late 1970s, equipped with a radar and used to train navigators in the art of using an airborne radar set. Appropriately, the flight that did this task was known as 1066 Flight.

Flying the Hastings was a complete change to flying the nimble, diminutive Gnat but, perched up high above the ground in the right-hand seat and acting as second pilot (untrained), I had a most enjoyable six weeks and notched up 42 hours' piston-engine flying time. We trundled around over Salisbury Plain disgorging parachutists and things called SEAC Containers – I was never sure what these were. There was also a gentle meander around the RAF's Mediterranean establishments – Luqa in Malta, Tripoli in Libya, Nicosia in Cyprus – all done at a steady 150 knots. Throughout my six weeks there I never was allowed to attempt a take-off or landing, a wise precaution under the circumstances as the Hastings had quite a reputation for being tricky close to the ground. You also had to be extremely strong, as the control loads were monumental when compared with a Gnat. I did, however, become very skilled in raising and lowering the undercarriage and flaps.

Then it was on to No. 231 OCU (Operational Conversion Unit) at RAF Bassingbourn, just north of Royston in Cambridgeshire. This was a delightful establishment where we were taught to fly that classic aircraft, the Canberra, another of W E Petter's designs. The OCU was equipped with the T4 version, where two pilots were squeezed into the space originally designed for one, so dual sorties were very chummy affairs. We flew our 'solo' sorties in the B2 version, which was no longer in any front-line squadron. The Canberra was a simple aircraft. The T4 and B2 had early Rolls-Royce Avon engines, which were very prone to compressor stall if mishandled and also prone to icing. The cockpit instrumentation was rather old fashioned, all the fuel was carried in three fuselage tanks and wing tip drop tanks, the flying controls were manually operated and the pilot sat under a goldfish bowl-like canopy, which could not be opened but gave an adequate view forwards and sideways, but none rearwards.

The aircraft had a good performance, and could operate up to 45,000 feet without difficulty but it got pretty cold at that altitude. It was limited to a maximum speed of 450 knots at low level, a speed it could exceed quite easily. At high level it suffered from compressibility effects with its straight, rather thick, wing and was limited to 0.8 M. Its flaps were very simple, down only with no intermediate setting, so they were only used for landing. It had a large bomb bay with hydraulically operated doors.

Inevitably, with its twin engines, much time was spent practising flying on one engine. This was an activity that could easily lead to trouble. Engine failure shortly after take-off resulted in a marked yaw and roll towards the failed engine, which had to be promptly controlled by opposite rudder and aileron. At low speeds the rudder loads were very heavy and the minimum speed that you could control the aircraft depended on your physical ability to hold on full rudder deflection. The taller and stronger brethren could hold the lowest speeds. One of the flying exercises was to determine your individual critical speed on one engine. This was done by flying at 1500 feet with one engine throttled back, reducing speed steadily with the other engine set to a high power setting.

Shortly before my arrival two instructors were practising this exercise together in a T4. The demonstrating instructor, a big Canadian on exchange duty, was holding a very high power setting at a nice, low speed. Unfortunately the top latch of his ejection seat was not done up properly and the action of him holding on full rudder pushed the seat up the rails to the point when it fired, throwing him out of the aircraft. This left an astonished non-flying instructor with the task of recovering the out of control Canberra and landing it, with a hole in the canopy, at the nearest airfield. The Canadian luckily survived this dramatic experience.

Single-engine circuits and landings were hard work and once flap had been selected you were committed to land. Roller landings were only permitted in the T4 with a QFI as the early Avons were tricky to accelerate evenly once throttled back on touchdown. The B2 had very primitive ejection seats that needed a minimum of 200 knots and 1000 feet to work, whereas the T4's seats were the standard 90-knot/ground-level seats like the Jet Provost's. Compared with the Gnat the Canberra felt somewhat old fashioned but it was a gentle aircraft that only bit if you took liberties with it, particularly on one engine.

I was crewed up with a navigator of vast experience, and girth, Flight Lieutenant Vic Avery, whose wisdom and common sense I valued enormously. He had flown Canberras before and I'm sure he monitored my youthful impetuosity and inexperience with great care and he kept me out of trouble on many occasions. The course consisted of general handling, including lots of practice engine failures and single-engine circuits; instrument flying, navigation at high and low level, night flying, a bit of formation and some basic aerobatics. These were used as a lead in to the Low Altitude Bombing System, or LABS, manoeuvre, which the operational aircraft used for nuclear weapon delivery. Just one visit was made to a weapons range for a session of medium-level bombing, a delivery mode that was not used on the front line any more. All told, it was an undemanding and gentlemanly course that allowed plenty of time off to go sailing. London was only one hour's drive away – what a change from Anglesey – and Cambridge a mere fifteen minutes' away. I enjoyed my time at Bassingbourn.

The course was 83 hours' of flying and when completed Vic and I were posted to No. 16 Squadron, RAF Laarbruch, in Germany close to the Dutch border. Training was now positively over and operational service on the front line now beckoned. I certainly hadn't been a star during training but I had survived reasonably well and the prospect of a nice tour abroad loomed before me, flying a classic aircraft. Before going out to Germany, I remember going to the SBAC Air Show at Farnborough and being very impressed by the brand new Blackburn Buccaneer Mk 2 – little realising then how much I would one day be involved with this splendid aircraft.

CHAPTER FOUR

The First Tour
– 1964 to 1966

No. 16 Squadron was a famous RAF unit, formed originally at St Omer in 1915. Its motto was *Operta Aperta*,
meaning 'hidden things will be revealed'. It was an
Army Co-operation squadron for most of the inter-war years
and the beginning of World War Two, then became a reconnaissance squadron equipped with Mustangs and Spitfires. After the
war it remained based in Germany and flew Vampires and
Venoms before being equipped with the Canberra B(I)8. Its role
as a light bomber squadron was primarily nuclear strike, with a
secondary role of conventional ground attack by day and night.

The Canberra B(I)8 was a two-seat version of the aircraft, specifically designed for ground attack and intruder missions. Unlike
the original Canberra, the pilot now sat behind and above the
navigator in a redesigned cockpit with a fighter-type bubble
canopy, which, for some inexplicable reason, could not be
opened. Thus it became extremely hot inside until one got
airborne and the cockpit conditioning started to work.

The navigator lived in a sort of tunnel, ahead of and below the
pilot. He had a small chart table for high-level navigation and a
couch in the nose to lie on for low-level navigation, looking out
through a transparent nose with two small side windows. He
had no ejection seat and relied on a manually operated para-

chute for escape, through the side entrance door. Most of our flying was at low level, but his chances of escape in an emergency at low level were slim. The pilot did have an ejection seat, but when I arrived on 16 Squadron it was still one of the earliest types with a limited operating envelope. During my tour it was replaced by a more modern seat with a ground capability at 90 knots.

The B(I)8 was equipped with more powerful Avon engines than the earlier B2 and carried considerably more fuel in integral tanks in the wings in addition to the three tanks in the fuselage. Wing tip tanks could also be fitted but there was a fairly low airspeed limit associated with them that inhibited any weapons delivery training so generally they were only used on long-range transit sorties. The cockpit layout was quite different and much improved on the B2 and T4. The aircraft had a simple fixed gunsight but no bombsight so traditional medium-level bomb delivery from straight and level flight was not possible. The rest of the systems were the same as the B2.

The two navigation aids fitted were a DECCA navigation system and a Doppler system called Blue Silk. DECCA used a series of ground stations to transmit signals that were displayed in the aircraft and transferred by the navigator to a chart, which was over-printed with a series of parabolic lines. It was a very accurate system but there was only a limited number of DECCA chains in existence, mainly in Europe. The Doppler Blue Silk was moderately accurate and displayed ground speed, drift and track; wind velocity could be derived from it. There was also a facility to drive a roller map from the Blue Silk, but this involved extensive preparation of long strips of map, which were quite narrow and thus limited in value. It was easy to disappear off the side of the map if you diverted off track. The roller map was a bit of a gimmick and was hardly ever used.

The B(I)8 had only two radios, a standard multi-frequency UHF set and a ten-channel preset VHF radio. It also had an Instrument Landing System (ILS), but surprisingly no radio compass. Thus our ability to navigate accurately outside the confines of the UK and Germany was limited. Overall, the B(I)8 was a big improvement on previous marks of Canberra, at least for the pilot. It was very nice to fly albeit rather heavy on the controls, and when on one engine could be more demanding than earlier models because of its increased weight and thrust. It was strange to be able to throw this large aircraft around doing what were essentially aerobatic manoeuvres from low level. Fatigue consumption was a constant worry, but it was a straight-forward aircraft with a proven record of reliability.

The general pattern of flying in RAF Germany was a mixture of navigation exercises at high and low level over Germany and the UK, with regular weapons sorties to the Ranges. The whole of Germany was divided into a series of low-flying areas linked by link routes in which the minimum height was 250 feet – outside the areas and link routes the minimum height was 500 feet, so it was one vast play area. The UK low-flying system was also a series of areas and link routes but low flying outside these was not permitted. Running down the centre of Germany was the border with East Germany with its associated Air Defence Identification Zone. Penetration of the ADIZ was not permitted and it was also protected by a Buffer Zone. Flight in the Buffer Zone was permitted but with care; if a 'Brass Monkeys' call was transmitted on the 'Guard' frequency any aircraft in the Buffer Zone hearing it was required immediately to turn west. One took great care when navigating near the border! The main weapons range was situated at Nordhorn, on the Dutch border in the north-west of Germany, but others were also available in the UK – Tain, Wainfleet – and for a while there was a French range we could use called Suippes.

The B(I)8's weapons were simple. For our primary nuclear strike role we used a tactical nuclear weapon of American origin. It filled the entire bomb bay. It was closely guarded by the Americans, who would only release it for actual use on the word of their President. There were therefore many American weapon custodians and guards at Laarbruch. The only delivery method was called Low Altitude Bombing System (LABS), an American system that had been developed to allow the delivery aircraft to approach at high speed and low level. The weapon was tossed forwards by the action of the aircraft pulling up into a loft manoeuvre. Once the weapon had been released the aircraft would escape by continuing the loft manoeuvre into a roll of the top of the loop and departing in the opposite direction as fast as possible.

There were two delivery modes, Normal or Alternate. In the

Normal mode you approached at low level at 434 knots, having previously selected an Initial Point (IP). A time to run before initiating the pull up manoeuvre was calculated, taking into account the head or tailwind component. As you overflew the IP, you pressed the trigger, which initiated a timer. Once the timer ran out, the LABS display gave you a pitch demand, which you followed, pulling about 3½ g. At 60 degrees of pitch the weapon was released, to fly onward for about 3 miles; you continued to pull over into a roll off the top of a loop and (hopefully) escaped in the opposite direction. In the Alternate mode, you flew to the target, then pressed the trigger. You then pulled up into your LABS manoeuvre but this time the weapon was released at 120 degrees of pitch. It flew upwards, then descended down onto the target whilst you again (hopefully) escaped after completing the roll off the top of the loop.

There was a switch in the pilot's cockpit, the Normal/Alternate switch, which selected the angle of pitch for weapon release. Needless to say, it was vital for this to be in the right position. Many a practice bomb was released inadvertently into Germany with the switch at Normal for an Alternate attack, and vice versa. Luckily our practice bombs were very small.

The LABS manoeuvre itself was quite an exciting thing to do in a fairly large aircraft from low level. You could get into real trouble if you pulled up too slackly, or allowed the nose to drop too much at the completion of the roll out at the end of the manoeuvre, as the Canberra would decelerate or accelerate very quickly. The accuracy of this type of attack was surprisingly good, given all the variables that affected it. We used to put bombs within 200 yards of the target on a regular basis, which was quite sufficient for an atom bomb.

In addition to the bombing ranges in Europe we also went regularly to Libya, where the weather was always much better, to carry out concentrated LABS work ups. There were two ranges, one at RAF El Adem, a remote base near Tobruk in east Libya, and another at a place called Tarhuna, a few miles south of Idris, where there was also an RAF Detachment.

LABS was our everyday bread and butter, because in those days NATO policy was for massive retaliation in the event of a Soviet incursion into West Germany. We would have 'gone nuclear' straight away. Most of our pre-planned targets were in Poland and the Baltic states, but there was also an option to deliver a nuclear weapon direct into the battlefield if called on to do so – a process called Selective Release. The ubiquitous 25-lb practice bomb was used to simulate a nuclear weapon and the B(I)8 could carry four, two on a carrier on each wing weapon pylon. Very occasionally clearance was given for a 'Shape' to be released. The 'Shape' was a concrete version of the real thing; it weighed the same and had the exact same profile but was filled with concrete rather than a nuclear warhead.

I recall being taken to Nordhorn Range within days of my arrival at Laarbruch to witness delivery of a Shape as the culmination of a Taceval Exercise. It was a gloomy day. The crew had been briefed to deliver the Shape in the Alternate mode so that those on the ground could see the whole event from the Range tower. Sure enough, right on time, the Canberra appeared out of the murk, bomb doors open, at high speed. It pulled up over the target but to everyone's amazement the huge Shape left the aircraft at about 60 degrees of pitch – the Normal/Alternate switch had been left in the wrong position! The Shape disappeared into Germany, never to be seen again. We returned to Laarbruch, glad that we had not been involved other than as spectators!

The first task for any new aircrew arriving from the OCU at Bassingbourn was to convert onto the B(I)8, then become familiar with flying in Germany. Once this aircraft and theatre conversion was complete there followed an intensive work up in the nuclear strike role; this often took some time because of poor weather and I spent two sessions at El Adem and Tarhuna during the winter of 1964/5 where the weather permitted the necessary minimum number of LABS bombing sorties to be completed. Once this work up was finished a new crew could go into QRA.

Quick Reaction Alert (QRA) had to be maintained for 365 days a year. This involved having two Canberras loaded with nuclear weapons and ready to start, at 15 minutes' notice to get airborne. Two crews, with the associated ground crews, RAF police guards, American weapon custodians and guards lived in the QRA Compound, which was close to the main runway threshold and surrounded by a high security fence. As I remember it, one spent two weeks on QRA, 24 hours on, 24 hours off. You often flew normal training sorties during your 24 hours off.

Life in the 'Pen', as it was known, followed a predictable routine. Each day the aircraft had to be checked out, you had to study and be fully familiar with your route and target, and of course you had to be able to get airborne within 15 minutes of the hooter sounding, which meant living permanently in flying kit. We used regularly to be brought up to 10 minutes' readiness, which meant being strapped in and ready to start, but we never got to the point where the engines were started.

Being on QRA was very boring, it seemed inconceivable that we would ever really be launched; if we had been, there would have been nothing to come back to. We became quite good at cooking exotic meals and playing various games. At that time there was no British TV available, only the BBC World Service. We also used to leave the occasional 'spoof' map lying around showing how we were planning to drop our nukes on America, to get the American custodians all excited.

Would we ever have been launched in the event of an outbreak of hostilities in Europe? It is very difficult to say. Doubtless the need for US and British permission would have been time consuming and difficult in times of tension. Not long after I left 16 Squadron, the Soviet Union put down a popular uprising in Czechoslovakia; tension increased considerably and QRA was doubled up. However, nobody had much idea what was going on because of the jamming of communications with Czechoslovakia, so in the end nothing more happened. It is interesting that after the Canberra was withdrawn from service and replaced by a combination of Phantom, Buccaneer, Jaguar and finally Tornado aircraft, nuclear QRA, with British weapons, was maintained virtually to the end of the RAF's time in Germany.

RAF Laarbruch was built in the early 1950s, right on the Dutch border. The remains of the Siegfried defence line, built by the Germans as the first line of defence for the Reich, ran through the area covered by the airfield; many of the trenches and old fortifications were still evident. There was a single runway and two parallel taxiways, which were available as standby emergency runways. In 1964 there were only two squadrons in residence, 16 and 31 (a Canberra PR unit), although there was room for another two. We lived in barrack blocks in single rooms, which were smaller than those I had lived in at Cranwell.

The reason for this was that the man in charge of building the airfield had charged for a full-size, standard NATO base, but had built Laarbruch to a smaller specification all round. He then pocketed the extra cash and put it into a Swiss bank account, which doubtless paid for a comfortable retirement once he had been released from jail. We had to live with the consequences: smaller rooms; a runway that was a little too short and too narrow; a ring road around the airfield that was only wide enough for one way traffic; a fence that kept people in rather than out. The list was endless. Nevertheless, our quality of life was excellent. Drink was very cheap in the Officers' Mess – it was cheaper to put vodka in one's car windscreen wash than buy anti-freeze stuff at a garage. Petrol was bought through a rationing system that gave us extremely preferential prices compared with the Germans and cars could be bought without incurring purchase tax. Compared with our colleagues in the UK we were very well off.

The secondary role of the Canberra B(I)8, the one that it had originally been designed for, was to provide long-range ground attack using conventional weapons by day or night. As this role was not part of the RAF's contribution to NATO, it was only practised twice a year on conventional weapons practice camps, usually lasting a month, and held overseas at Akrotiri in Cyprus or Luqa in Malta. Our conventional armoury was very primitive and dated from the World War Two era. A gun pack containing four 20-mm cannon was fitted into the rear half of the bomb bay; each gun had a maximum of 500 rounds of ammunition which gave a very long firing time. The sighting system was a very simple ring and bead type gunsight, which could not be depressed or deflected to take wind effect into account. The front half of the bomb bay could carry sixteen 4.5-inch flares, most of which had been made in the late 1930s. These were to illuminate targets at night. A grand total of two 1000-lb bombs could be carried, one on each wing pylon. The only method of delivery was from a shallow-dive attack, again using the primitive gunsight. Although it was theoretically possible to fit three 1000-lb bombs in the front half of the bomb bay, they would not fall clear if delivered in a dive attack, as the Canberra did not have explosive release units to push the bombs out. There was no facility to deliver bombs from level flight as we did not have a bombsight. Thus the front half of the bomb bay was always used for flares.

Our attempts at gunnery were fairly accurate from 10-degree dive attacks and some good scores could be obtained. Shallow dive bombing from a 30-degree dive attack was somewhat 'hit and miss' as the target virtually disappeared under the nose at the release point. Our ability to hit targets at night under the fitful light of the ancient 4.5-inch flares was minimal. Nevertheless, we all enjoyed conventional weapon delivery enormously, although we did not get many opportunities to practise. Events in the Far East were to change this during my tour on 16 Squadron.

In January 1965, after I had been on the squadron for four months, the squadron was stood down from its Quick Reaction Alert (QRA) commitment so that it could deploy to the Far East, in the conventional role. The British were involved in a little local difficulty between the newly emergent ex-colonies that had become Malaysia and Indonesia. This became known as the 'Indonesian Confrontation'. Most of the action took place on the ground, high in the jungled mountain border areas of Borneo. But after (rumour had it) a Russian-built 'Badger' bomber had flown down the runway at Kuching with its bomb doors open and other mildly tiresome provocations, the whole thing showed some promise of becoming moderately entertaining in the air. Despite the size of the RAF's Far East Air Force, which had eighteen operational squadrons, further detachments were sent out to Malaya and Singapore from the UK, Germany and Cyprus. Australia and New Zealand also sent operational squadrons.

No. 16 Squadron was deployed to an up country bare base airfield called Kuantan – about half way up the east coast of Malaya. As I was still the most junior member of the squadron I was given to the tender mercies of RAF Transport Command for my journey to Malaya. I was bumped off the Britannia at RAF Muharraq (Bahrain) in favour of a more senior officer, so I spent four days there, of which I only have a hazy recollection before the next transport aircraft – a Comet – came through. Most of the time was spent in the Mess bar playing a form of cricket with the resident members of 8 and 208 Squadrons, the Middle East Air Force Hunter Wing. The 'batsman' threw an empty beer can into a rapidly rotating ceiling fan – there was no air conditioning in those days; if the can was subsequently caught by one of the 'fielders' he was declared out and had to buy a round.

Kuantan had a 2000-yard runway, a dispersal area but no taxiway and no permanent buildings or facilities other than a single-storey wooden terminal building with a small veranda on top for Air Traffic Control, to serve the Malaysian Airlines Dakota that flew in every other day. The nearest diversion airfield was in Singapore, 160 miles away. There was only a single telephone line to communicate with the outside world, an operation made more difficult by the fact that you had to talk to a Chinese telephonist to get connected to anyone outside. Communications security was non-existent.

There wasn't much space between the runway and the jungle but what there was, was filled by a variety of leaky tents dating from World War Two in which we lived, slept, ate and briefed. Sanitation was provided by some cold water taps and a local gentleman, who would arrive every morning driving a tractor towing a bomb trolley carrying clean Elsans and buckets, which he removed again in the evening. We were soon convinced that the real (secret) reason behind our presence at Kuantan was to carry out the field trial of the 'Closet, chemical lightweight tropical', or Elsan. It failed. The seat cracked under the weight of anyone over 8 stone. The crack opened up when you sat down, which was fine – but when you stood up. . .ouch! There were a few strategically positioned slit trenches, which made excellent baths since they filled up with rain every afternoon when the duty storm arrived. These were invisible to the uninitiated when full (before they put the sand bags round them). Having politely directed some visiting senior staff officer through the pouring rain to his tent, young officers would watch his retreating bush jacket and 'Dollar Brolly' (an exquisitely intricate piece of engineering in wood, string and oiled paper), with collective bated breath, praying that he would find one of the trenches on his way there.

There were also some rather elderly 20-mm Oerlikon anti-aircraft guns, which had been dug out of Singapore Naval Dockyard, scattered about to provide airfield defence. All lesser mortals (ie non-aircrew) were 'trained' in the use of these guns in the event of an air raid. But to cock the bloody thing you had to strap your heaviest man in the harness, and the rest of the team had to swing on his legs, grunting and swearing, in order to compress the biggest spring I have ever seen. By the time the gun was finally loaded and ready to fire the enemy bomber pilot would be back home addressing his after flight Nasi Goreng.

Food was provided from a single cookhouse, made of wooden frames, canvas and the odd bit of aluminium sheet. The quality of the food, all purchased locally, was surprisingly good. Unfortunately the cookhouse burnt down during a visit from the Command Fire Officer, giving him a graphic demonstration of our fire-fighting ability, and its replacement was never quite as good.

Flying operations were delightfully straightforward. There were a couple of air traffic controllers, a mobile DF and a radio, but that was all. A mobile air defence radar was flown up at one point during our detachment, but I don't recall it ever offering much of a service. Eventually it was taken away. Our version of the Canberra had navigation aids that were optimised for use in Germany and there were no spare parts for them in the Far East. Consequently, after about two weeks we were dependent solely on our trusty navigators, trusty stopwatches and some in-different, untrustworthy maps for our navigational accuracy around a fairly hostile environment. Apart from the occasional burst tyre and bird strike our safety record was incident free, apart from one heart-stopping moment when a crew experienced a double engine surge in the circuit at night, caused by rain water ingress into the fuel system. They were downwind in the inky black when it occurred and the runway was already occupied by another aircraft backtracking for take-off. Luckily our plucky crew managed to recover one engine and arrived on finals just as the runway became clear. Remember, the navigator had no ejection seat in this mark of Canberra.

We were tasked to provide long-range day and night dive bombing and strafing with 1000-lb bombs and 20-mm cannon, illuminating targets at night with our ancient 4.5-inch flares. The likely targets were mainly airfields on the island of Java. The only weapons range where we were allowed to practise the night delivery profiles was China Rock Range, but because of its proximity to the Jahor Baharu coastline and jungle area where Indonesian paratroops were reported to have infiltrated, the Range Safety Officer and his party were evacuated every night, so we used the 'Clear Range' procedure for weapon delivery. This meant that the responsibility for ensuring that it was safe to drop weapons rested with the aircrew of the delivery aircraft.

On the first night of flare dropping and gunnery on China Rock our most experienced crew were sent off to try out the procedures. They duly scattered numerous flares over what they thought was the weapons range but never succeeded in identifying the target, due to a combination of lack of aircraft nav aids and the absence of the Range Safety Officer. They must have been some way off the target because their flares' parachutes all ended up in the jungle on the mainland, causing a major security alert as the locals thought that some very small Indonesian guerrillas, or some supplies for infiltrators, had been delivered. The Headquarters of the Far East Air Force was not amused!

Night flying from Kuantan was challenging. In that airfield lighting was provided by a very feeble and unreliable set of electric lights supplemented by gooseneck flares, a galvanised watering can that had a huge paraffin-fed wick. The goosenecks were much brighter than the electric lights but there were only enough of them to put down one side of the runway. This made night approaches particularly interesting if you had forgotten on which side of the runway the goosenecks were.

The squadron's only moment of glory came one morning when we were tasked to strafe an area of jungle where the aforementioned Indonesian infiltrators were reputed to be hiding. Given that it was daylight the area was attacked successfully. What result this had we never did discover, but Indonesian infiltration of the mainland petered out over the subsequent months.

Off-duty amusements were simple. Every afternoon a 3-ton lorry would set off for the local beach – Paradise Beach – which was idyllic and unspoilt. It has now been developed into a Club Med holiday complex. The local town of Kuantan was a classic example of a Malay trading community unchanged since the Edwardian era. Great logs of timber were rolled into the waters of the muddy river, to be loaded by hand onto sail-powered cargo vessels, which then transported them down the coast to Singapore. There was a busy market full of live animals, any goods you could imagine and exotic tropical smells. The architecture was straight out of the nineteenth century and there was not a skyscraper in sight; now the town is a mass of high-rise development. There was one small hotel called the Nan Yang, which was entered through a pair of swing doors that looked as if were straight out of a Wild West film set. The Kuantan Massage Parlour provided the services one would expect; the only other place of entertainment was the Kuantan Club. This was straight out of a Somerset Maughan novel. It had an air of seedy colonial gentility and was full of stale cigar smoke in which the dwindling number of ex-pat planters met to bemoan their passing sway – whilst swaying over a large whisky 'stengah'. There was an open-air cinema screen on the airfield's domestic site where scratchy old films were occasionally shown. Every so often an aircraft was allowed to go away to Singapore for the weekend where the crew enjoyed the delights of civilisation, air conditioning and Bugis Street.

Eventually it was time to go back to Laarbruch. I was No. 2 to the Boss for the return flight, which was to route via Butterworth, Gan, Bahrain, Akrotiri and Luqa. Gan was a tiny coral atoll in the Indian Ocean with a single runway from one end to the other and no diversion airfield within hundreds of miles. The long flight from Butterworth involved trying to climb above the intertropical convergence zone, an area of thick high cloud and vicious thunderstorms – an unpleasant experience. It was a great relief to see Gan, and a greater one to turn off the single runway without any drama.

During the leg to Bahrain the Boss announced that his section was diverting to Masirah, a very remote RAF staging post on an island on the south-east tip of the Oman. There seemed no obvious reason for this but as I was still a very inexperienced No. 2 I did not think to question this decision. After clearing the itinerant donkeys and camels from Masirah's runway by a series of low passes we landed. I asked the Boss's navigator why we had diverted to this barren outpost of the Empire when all had seemed to be going well. He replied 'Because this is where you can buy the best desert boots in the world and the Boss and I need a new pair.' It seemed a fair decision. We rejoined the rest of the squadron at Bahrain after flying over a very inhospitable-looking Oman, played some more beer can cricket, then flew uneventfully over Iran and Turkey to Akrotiri, Luqa and finally Laarbruch, where we arrived as a nine-ship formation, all without much in the way of nav aids. It was overall a great experience.

Somehow, looking back on it all, it looks disgracefully 'gash' from a modern professional standpoint. But the lack of good communications and nav aids, and living in a welter of confusion, made everyone conscious of basic principles. It induced in people a level of alert scepticism, such that they could always successfully 'cuff' it when the grand plan went awry. Not bad training for war – and not a management plan, budget holder, accountant or business consultant in sight! Just before we left we commissioned some Selangor pewter beer tankards to commemorate our Far East experience. Mine is inscribed simply 'JP [for Junior Pilot] XVI, Kuantan '65'. It is still in regular use.

In retrospect, it seems extraordinary that our conventional capability was so primitive. The Canberra B(I)8 carried the same weapon load as a World War Two ground attack fighter, the only improvement being the ability to carry considerably more rounds of ammunition. Weapon aiming was very basic and the ability to attack targets at night with any accuracy was minimal. The development costs of the V force and the nuclear deterrent had probably starved other more conventional tactical elements of the RAF of any improvements. This situation was only remedied with the cancellation of TSR2, the transfer of responsibility for the nuclear deterrent to the Royal Navy and the introduction of tactical aircraft such as the Harrier, Jaguar, Phantom and Buccaneer into the RAF.

After this experience of the Far East and a semi-operational environment, life back at Laarbruch seemed rather mundane. The squadron soon settled down back into its normal routine, QRA was resumed and trips around the Mediterranean RAF bases resumed, along with bombing detachments to Libya. The only real bit of excitement that I recall was on a visit to Gibraltar in the summer of 1965, when I was intercepted in the visual circuit pattern by a Spanish Air Force F86 Sabre fighter, which followed me around the Rock in close formation, without doing anything else aggressive. As the Spanish were putting more and more pressure on Gibraltar at this time it was a slightly unnerving incident and I was glad to get on the ground safely.

The squadron had an excellent conventional weapons detachment to Akrotiri, Cyprus, in January 1966. I recall being the Range Safety Officer at Larnaca Range (now the civil airport), and having great difficulty in keeping the local Turkish population off the range. They would gather in large crowds and rush onto the range area to collect the brass shell cases, which were ejected from each aircraft as it fired its cannon. They were so keen to get these shell cases that they would chase the aircraft as it fired and try to catch the cases as they fell to the ground. Injury was frequent and inevitably we would be blamed for the consequences. We therefore resorted to firing flares at them from our Very pistols in an attempt to keep them away until after the aircraft had ceased firing. This tactic proved to be moderately successful.

On the squadron's return to Laarbruch at the end of January 1966, I discovered that the Royal Navy were seeking volunteers from the RAF to fly Sea Vixen and Buccaneer aircraft with the Fleet Air Arm, as there was a shortage of RN pilots. At this time the government was in the process of threatening to abolish conventional aircraft carriers so this seemed like an excellent opportunity to experience a form of aviation that looked as if it would soon be extinct. I therefore applied to fly Buccaneers in the strike role. The rest of the squadron thought I was mad, but it also offered another escape route from the possibility of a posting to the V Force, where many Canberra pilots were sent for their second tour.

I was delighted to discover that my application was accepted and I was to report to RNAS Lossiemouth, in the north of Scotland, in July 1966 for a swept wing conversion course on the Hunter before starting the Buccaneer Operational Flying Course. During my twenty months on 16 Squadron I accumulated a total of 526 hours on the Canberra, I was lucky enough to have been all round the Middle East and experienced an operational detachment to the Far East. It was a good background with which to go off on loan service to the Senior Service, where the highest standards would doubtless be expected. So I packed my bits and pieces into a Canberra and delivered them to Lossiemouth. I then hitched my Mirror dinghy to the back of my Triumph Spitfire sports car, and set off on the long journey from Germany to the north of Scotland, looking forward to something completely different but with happy memories of my first tour.

CHAPTER FIVE

The Fleet Air Arm
– 1966 to 1968

R oyal Naval Air Station Lossiemouth was a very different place to RAF Laarbruch. Situated in wonderful country-side on the shores of the Moray Firth, it was a very busy airfield. It was the original stone frigate – you lived in a cabin in the Wardroom, phone calls from off base were announced as shore telephone calls, the liberty boat (bus) left the gangway (main gate) for Elgin. The floor was the deck and the ceiling the deckhead – all in all a very confusing environment for someone from the RAF but you had to learn quickly if you were to be accepted by the Royal Navy. This was a difficult time in that the government of the day was clearly intent on getting rid of aircraft carriers in favour of land-based RAF aircraft, so relations between the Fleet Air Arm and the RAF were not always harmonious. Thankfully there were no hard feelings between the light and dark blue at my lowly rank level.

I started off by doing a short conversion course on the Hunter with 764 Naval Air Squadron (NAS), which reintroduced me to swept wing handling techniques and naval aviation practices. The two variants of Hunter used by the Fleet Air Arm were the T8 and the GA11. Royal Navy policy was not to waste front-line combat aircraft by making trainer versions, so the ubiquitous Hunter T8 served as the training aircraft for the Scimitar, Sea Vixen and Buccaneer. Compared with the Gnat, the Hunter T8 was a simple aircraft. It was powered by the same version of the Avon engine as the Canberra B(I)8, which gave some 7500 lb thrust at sea level. It carried 3000 lb of internal fuel, nearly always augmented by two 100-gallon drop tanks, which increased the fuel state to 4900 lb (not a great amount but better than the Gnat). Its power controls were very light and easy to use. Manual reversion was much more straightforward than with the Gnat, just rather heavy. None of the Royal Navy's Hunters carried a gun but they could carry practice bombs and rockets. The single-seat GA11 version was essentially a Hunter F4 with the gun pack removed and the same wing as the T8, with the saw tooth leading edge. Both versions had arrestor hooks for use with airfield arrestor cables. A few of the T8s were equipped with the OR 946 Integrated Flight Instrument System, as fitted to the Buccaneer, which Folland had claimed couldn't be fitted in a Hunter! I spent three carefree weeks flying Hunters with 764 NAS relearning some old techniques. Then it was over to 736 NAS, the Buccaneer operational flying training squadron, for conversion to the Buccaneer.

After the relative simplicity of the Canberra, the Buccaneer was altogether a much more complex aircraft. It was designed and manufactured by the Blackburn Aircraft Company and was the company's first ever jet-powered combat aircraft. It was a big beast, with a 44-foot wingspan and a length of 60 feet. Its original role was to deliver a nuclear weapon against Russian capital ships, but it was also a very capable conventional attack aircraft and it could deliver a wide range of weapons. It had to fly at high subsonic speeds at very low level, which it did extremely well, but it also had to fly slowly enough to be launched and recovered from the rather small Royal Navy aircraft carriers, thus it presented quite a challenge to its designers. It was extremely robust in order to cope with the stresses of high-speed, low-level flight, many of the components being milled out of solid billets of aluminium, an entirely new construction technique at that time. It used the 'Area Rule', a design concept that reduced drag at high speed and as a consequence the fuselage had a very distinctive 'Coca-Cola' bottle shape with a large bulge behind the wings. This had the advantage of providing plenty of room for the complex avionics, which were all valve driven. The swept, folding wings were equipped with sophisticated high lift devices to enable the aircraft to be catapult launched and to fly slowly enough to land back on board a carrier.

The ailerons could be drooped through 25 degrees to act as additional flaps, whilst retaining their differential roll control function. The small flaps on the inboard, non-folding, section of the wing, could be lowered through 45 degrees and the entire wing/aileron/flap area was 'blown' with high pressure air. This was known as Boundary Layer Control, or BLC. It delayed the stalling speed and allowed the approach speed to be reduced to a minimum of 127 knots. It was essential to have BLC on at aileron droop angles beyond 10 degrees or the wing would stall. Unfortunately the action of drooping the ailerons produced a very strong nose down trim change, so, to counteract this, an electrically operated flap on the tailplane was moved through the same angle as the ailerons but in the opposite direction. The entire undersurface of the tailplane was also 'blown'. Synchronisation of aileron droop/tailplane flap was essential; if more than 10 degrees' difference occurred between the two, longitudinal control would be lost. There were displays in the cockpit showing the relative positions of these control surfaces; they looked a bit like a section of round cheese when they moved so inevitably were known as the 'cheeses'. The whole system seemed incredibly complex but it worked very well, provided you made sure that the aileron droop and tailplane flap always stayed synchronised and that the BLC system was on auto.

The Buccaneer carried most of its fuel in eight integral fuselage tanks, connected in pairs; the fuel was fed to the engines by hydraulically driven pumps known as proportioners. These kept the fuel flow from the tanks correct so that the aircraft's centre of gravity remained constant. The Buccaneer was equipped with a fixed air-to-air refuelling probe; the original design was retractable but it proved to be too short so was replaced by a longer, fixed installation.

There was also a hydraulic system that powered the general services such as landing gear, hook, wing folding, the bomb door operation, the airbrake, the wheel brakes and the flaps. This was probably the least reliable system in the aircraft; it operated at 4000 psi so inevitably suffered from numerous leaks. In the event of a leak the system shut itself down, leaving you with only single selections of essential services. The flying controls were hydraulically powered by separate systems that were very reliable. The aircraft had full auto stabilisation in all three axes and a standby yaw damper. It also had a fairly basic auto pilot with heading, barometric height and Mach number holds.

The two-man crew were accommodated under a long canopy, the Observer being seated higher and slightly off set from the pilot so he had a good view forwards.

The pilot's main instrument display was the OR 946 Integrated Flight Instrument System (IFIS) combined with a mass of more conventional instruments showing fuel state by individual tank, blow pressures, hydraulic pressures, electrical system status and radio altitude. There were also standby flight instruments that displayed airspeed, attitude, heading and height in the event of IFIS failure. The IFIS display of airspeed was not considered accurate enough for deck operations so a two-needle airspeed indicator (ASI) was stuck up on the coaming in the pilot's line of sight to give accurate speed indications for deck landings. Most of the weapons system controls were also in the front cockpit. Right in front of the pilot was the head up display (HUD), known as the Strike Sight, which displayed all the information needed to carry out an automatic or manual attack. Its glass could be lowered flat to improve the view forward, a Godsend when performing deck landings in poor visibility or into the sun.

Another device worthy of mention is the Airstream Direction Detector, or ADD. This was a small probe that stuck out from the side of the fuselage, with a series of slots cut in it. It was free to rotate so aligned itself with the relative airflow, thereby measuring the aircraft's angle of attack at any speed. It was capable of generating audio tones that varied as the angle of attack, and therefore the airspeed, changed. It was calibrated to generate a steady tone at the correct angle of attack/airspeed for final approach, with a high-pitched interrupted tone if the speed was too high and a loud, low interrupted tone if it was too low. It enabled the final approach to be flown entirely with one's head out of the cockpit, there being no need to check one's airspeed by looking at the ASI. It was a marvellous aid to deck launches and landings and also an invaluable warning device that the aircraft was approaching maximum performance.

The Observer had control of the navigation systems and the fire control radar, known as 'Blue Parrot', which was located in the nose. This was a powerful radar designed to detect and lock on to ship targets; it had a range of nearly 200 miles from high altitude. It provided range, bearing and closing speed information to the weapon system computer, enabling automatic toss attacks to be carried out using conventional or nuclear weapons. It also had a very limited mapping capability over land. The aircraft also had a Doppler navigation system called 'Blue Jacket', a device known as a Wide Band Homer that could detect radar transmissions and the usual radio equipment, including a long-range HF transmitter/receiver. Thus the Buccaneer was a very complex aircraft by comparison with the Canberra, but also a very capable and effective weapons system.

The Buccaneer was produced in three versions, the S1, the S2 and the S50, an export version of the S2 built for the South African Air Force. The S1 version was built in relatively small numbers and in 1966 was being steadily replaced by the S2, however, 736 NAS was still equipped mainly with the S1.

The S1's engines were Gyron Juniors, which were rather unreliable and short of thrust. Like all turbojets the Gyron Junior had a variable position intake guide vane system, but it was very sensitive and regularly got into the wrong position for the demanded RPM. There were even Inlet Guide Vane (IGV) position indicators in the cockpit, something I have never seen in any other aircraft. If the IGVs got into the wrong position the engine would stall or flame out, a regular occurrence. When the BLC system was selected extra fuel was applied to the engine in an attempt to offset the large loss of thrust. Cooling valves (Turbine Cooling Valves – TCVs) in the turbine assembly opened to provide a supply of cooling air to the inside of the turbine blades. This cooling air was essential to prevent failure of the turbine at high temperatures. So what with unreliable IGVs and TCVs that were essential with the BLC system, engine handling was complex. Even unblown take-offs were very slow events and in the blown approach configuration the aircraft was distinctly underpowered.

The S1's electrical system was also complicated. It used an air-driven alternator (Air Turbine Alternator – ATA) to provide the majority of AC services, the air being taken from the engines. If you throttled back excessively in flight the ATA would trip off line as the engine RPM reduced, depriving you of many essential AC services just when you really needed them. Thus operating the Buccaneer S1 was a challenging business and I'm glad I never had to go to sea with it.

The S2 was powered by Rolls-Royce Speys, which had nearly twice the thrust of the Gyron Junior, and were much more reliable, so as a consequence it was a much more sprightly performer. The S2 also had a much better and more reliable electrical system, and was really quite a different aircraft. Unusually, the S1 handled much better than the S2 in spite of its lack of thrust. It could actually achieve a higher maximum speed (whilst consuming fuel at a vast rate) than the S2 because of the small size of its air intakes and it was much less sensitive in pitch at high angles of attack and low speed. Nevertheless the S2 was a vastly superior aircraft, with a tremendous range and weapon-carrying capability. It was trickier to operate from the deck but was clearly a much safer and effective aircraft overall. The Buccaneer was the first jet aircraft designed exclusively for the Royal Navy from the outset rather than being some cast off from industry that the RAF didn't want, so it was very much the star of the Fleet Air Arm in the 1960s.

There were eight of us on our conversion course. The two naval pilots were Robin Cox (until recently Airbus chief pilot with Virgin) and Rory Neilsen, sadly killed later in a winter sports accident. The two naval observers were John Bennet (a chopped pilot) and 'Bodger' Reardon (an ex-Sea Vixen observer). The other four were all RAF, two navigators (Barry Titchen and Norman Roberson) and two pilots, Tim Cockerell (ex-Hunters) and me. I was crewed up with 'Bodger' for the duration of the course, an interesting and enlightening experience.

The course itself was demanding. Initial conversion to the aircraft was a challenge in that there was no dual control version so your first sortie was your first solo, with a QFI in the back seat offering advice on handling, often in no uncertain terms! Once type conversion was complete it was straight into navigation, formation, weapons system handling and weapon delivery sorties on the two local weapons ranges at Tain and Rosehearty. Then came a busy session of practice deck landings on the runway, known as 'MADDLs' (Mirror Assisted Dummy Deck

Landings). The runway was marked out in the same way as a carrier flight deck with a projector sight alongside. However, you could not get the feel of what it really would be like, since whatever you did the runway never moved, was always 8000 feet long and 150 feet wide and never pitched up and down. The target area for landing was roughly the size of a tennis court – not very big. You had to be right on the centre line and accurate to within 1 knot of speed, and you had to fly the glide path with total concentration. You made no attempt to flare; you simply flew the aircraft into the ground in an attempt to move the earth from its orbit. Initially I did not find this new technique easy to grasp. As I was struggling to master MADDLs, HMS *Hermes* sailed into the Moray Firth so we all had to go off and do some real DLP (Deck Landing Practice).

The first time you see an aircraft carrier from the air your immediate reaction is that it is quite impossible to land on it as it is far too small. Nevertheless we were all briefed and awaited our turn at DLP. The exercise did not start too well as one of the naval pilots on the course ahead tightened his final turn excessively, lost control and both he and his observer ejected – successfully. I had the greatest difficulty in mastering the technique until rescued by the RAF QFI on 736 NAS, Graham Smart. He realised I was not coping, took me to the deck first in a Hunter then in a Buccaneer (with him bravely in the back seat), and finally it clicked and I had no further problems. During this session of DLP none of us actually hooked on, so this experience still awaited us. Deck landing in a large aircraft like the Buccaneer on a small Royal Navy carrier was always a very challenging event and it never became a relaxed affair.

There only remained the requirement to experience a catapult (cat) shot. There was a shore catapult installation at the research establishment at Bedford and so three of us went down there to do three cat shots before going to sea. The catapult at Bedford was an amazing device, with a large adjacent boiler house that looked like a Chinese laundry generating the required quantities of steam. You taxied up a ramp onto the catapult itself and were fired off down a disused runway, which had a large barrier like a tennis net to stop you if the catapult didn't give you enough flying speed. Because there was no ship-generated head wind you always got a very fierce kick from this land-based device.

The technique used for launching a Buccaneer was 'hands off'. A tailplane trim setting was calculated, taking into account the aircraft's weight, centre of gravity, configuration and expected end speed after launch. This was set and the theory was that it would rotate the aircraft into the correct attitude for the initial climb without intervention from the pilot. Once positioned on the catapult the aircraft would be tensioned up, with its retractable tail skid resting on the deck. The pilot would apply full power and when happy, lock his left arm behind the throttles to ensure they remained at full power, raise his right hand to accept the launch then place it on his right thigh close to but not holding the control column. The catapult would fire after a short delay. The acceleration was phenomenal (0 to 120 knots in about 1½ seconds) and then everything stopped as you became airborne. It was like being fired into jelly. You then carefully took control by grasping the control column, retracted the landing gear and allowed the aircraft to accelerate to a safe climbing speed, retracting the aileron droop/flap combination in stages. Loss of an engine or boundary layer control air would mean instant ejection. The aircraft was very sensitive in pitch and it was important not to apply a large nose-up control input until a safe speed had been achieved.

There had been a number of incidents when Buccaneer S2s had pitched up rapidly on launch. One aircraft had been lost under these circumstances, so there was much debate as to whether squadron pilots were taking control too soon and inducing pitch up by over rotating. Eventually a very senior naval test pilot was sent to HMS *Victorious* to re-brief the pilots and to demonstrate a launch in the configuration claimed to be the most susceptible to pitch up. An unwilling volunteer was strapped into the back seat and the rest of the squadron aircrew went out to watch the launch. Luckily there were at least three plane guard helicopters in attendance. The aircraft immediately pitched up violently after launch, the crew ejected and were back on board within minutes. The test pilot did have the grace to admit that there was a problem! Changes were made to the launch procedures, the wing tanks' profile was changed so that they generated less lift and a more accurate tailplane indicator was fitted. These changes were successful and launching the Buccaneer S2 became much safer.

Cat shots were always exciting and if something went wrong

the only option was ejection. There was an underwater escape facility fitted to the ejection seat, which, if selected, would release you from the seat and propel you upward if you went into the sea still in the aircraft. However, the canopy had to be jettisoned first and most of us thought that we would come up right under the ship, not a healthy prospect. Few people bothered to have it switched on. On my final cat shot at Bedford I had a full fuel load for the return to Lossiemouth. The cat gave me such a powerful kick that the entire head up display became detached and fell in my lap!

One final exercise had to be completed, a session in the 'Dunker'. For this exercise a facsimile of an aircraft cockpit, with you strapped into it, would be lowered underwater to a depth of about 30 feet. Then you had to escape. This was done in the submarine escape training tower in Gosport. It is quite an interesting and unnerving experience, being lowered into deep water strapped into an aircraft cockpit!

By December 1966 I was deemed ready to join a front-line squadron. I had some 65 hours in the Buccaneer (only 13 in the Mk2), seven deck landings and two cat shots under my belt. I was posted to 801 NAS, HMS *Victorious*, at that time in the Far East. No. 801 was the first squadron to be equipped with the Buccaneer Mk2 and *Victorious* was half way through her commission, so I would be joining an experienced outfit.

The trip out to Singapore was just as slow as the previous one in 1965, however, this time I was going to a completely unknown environment. I remember finally arriving in the naval dockyard, late in the evening after a long, hot journey, and seeing the carrier for the first time. From the dockside she looked enormous. I found my way to the aft gangway, the one used by officers. No one seemed to be expecting me, but I was taken down to the Wardroom in the bowels of the ship, to discover that all the air squadrons were disembarked to the various airfields in Singapore and only ship's officers were currently on board. Nevertheless they filled me up with Horse's Neck (brandy and dry ginger) and eventually a cabin was found for me, even deeper inside the ship. I had no idea where I was and fell asleep, only to wake sometime later urgently needing to have a pee. I stumbled around the passageways and eventually found the heads (lavatories). Much relieved, I then tried to find my cabin again. I became totally lost, and, clad only in my underpants, had almost given up all hope of ever finding my cabin again when I walked past an open door and recognised my baggage! What a relief.

The next day I was collected by someone from the squadron and taken over to RAF Changi, where the squadron was located, a much more familiar environment. Many of the squadron personnel had returned to the UK for Christmas, but those who remained were having a very pleasant time living in the Fairey Point Officers' Mess, considerably more luxurious than HMS *Victorious*. The Officers' beach club was just around the corner, another fine establishment. The flesh pots of downtown Singapore were only a short taxi ride away and I seem to remember that we all took full advantage of them.

However, re-embarkation day moved ever closer. We spent our time airborne performing lots of 'MADDLs' at Changi by way of preparation. Finally, one morning the ship steamed past us as we sat at the beach club and that afternoon we launched to recover on board. The ship succeeded in finding the only piece of the South China Sea where there was a big swell and after a few hairy attempts to get on board we were all sent back to Changi.

The next morning conditions were much calmer and after three rollers I was told to put my hook down. I will never forget my first arrested landing; the deceleration was amazing but even more alarming was the urgency with which you were marshalled away from the angled flight deck to your parking spot, often with only the sea in view. Having finally shut down and climbed out, I looked around. Normally, after landing at an airfield and getting out, all relative motion has ceased and this is what you expect to see. By now, though, the ship was turning out of wind; I looked up, expecting the world to be still but the horizon was moving rapidly. It was so disorientating that I had to clutch hold of the aircraft ladder to stop myself falling over.

There now followed a period of intensive work-up training for the new members of the ship's crew and the new aircrew. We flew on average about twice a day. Finding one's way around the labyrinth of passageways and compartments was quite a challenge, especially as the older hands seemed to know their way around with unerring accuracy. I recall one occasion when, trying to remain inconspicuous in the Wardroom one evening, the Squadron Commander collared me to take a message to the operations room in the island. At that time the only way I knew how to get there was to go out onto the flight deck and walk along it to the island. So I set off, in the dark. As I climbed up the access ladder that led to the flight deck, something made me look to my right. There I saw a Sea Vixen on short finals; the other squadron was night flying and the flight deck was very active. Had I not turned to have a look I would have been flattened by it landing on. I retreated to the Wardroom – the message was not delivered. An aircraft carrier was a very dangerous place for the inexperienced.

Life on board soon settled down as we found our way around and got used to the routine. The flying was probably the most exciting and demanding that I have ever experienced. We started the day early, first launch usually being at 0700 hrs, which meant getting up at 0500 hrs, breakfast in the Aircrew Refreshment Buffet (ACRB) at 0530 hrs – always greasy fried eggs – then briefing at 0600 hrs. The aircraft would be ranged on the flight deck in order of launching – normally the Gannet AEW aircraft first, then the Buccaneers and last of all the Sea Vixens.

After start up the aircraft was taxied forward to the catapult and positioned accurately with the use of the Calley gear, inward-rotating rollers that ensured the aircraft was aligned exactly in the centre of the catapult. The hold back, which was a frangible metal link connected to the rear of the aircraft, was then connected to the deck. The aircraft's wings were then spread and the catapult bridle attached; the catapult shuttle was then moved forwards so that the aircraft was then tensioned up on the catapult in the flying attitude. On receipt of the clearance to launch from Flyco, the Flight Deck Officer (FDO) would give the wind up signal; once the pilot signalled that he was happy to launch the FDO would drop his green flag and the catapult would fire after a short pause.

Once airborne and joined up as a formation we would practise a variety of activities. Ship attack profiles, navigation exercises, weapon delivery work, air-to-air refuelling, battle formation and air combat, and strikes on coastal or inland targets all featured regularly. The ship tended to operate either close to Malaya or the Philippines, there being excellent

American facilities in the Philippines, including the enormous naval support facility at Subic Bay.

I was lucky enough to be selected not only to deliver a'Red Beard' 2000-lb nuclear weapon Shape on a 'Long Toss' attack on Tabones Range in the Philippines, but also to fire Bullpup missiles at Scarborough Shoal, an offshore reef with a wreck that made a suitable target. The 'Red Beard' was the British tactical nuclear weapon of that period, designed as the principal anti-ship weapon for the Buccaneer. It filled the entire bomb bay. The target was a small rocky island and the enormous bomb hit it right in the middle – a very satisfying experience. The Bullpup was a small air-to-surface missile of US origin, with a range of about 3 to 4 miles. It was fired in a shallow dive and controlled by the pilot, using a small control handle. It was a difficult missile to control accurately and much practice was needed on the very simple simulator that we had on board. On one occasion I recovered to the ship after failing to fire a Bullpup owing to bad weather. After landing on, the missile broke free from the aircraft and careered off down the flight deck, narrowly missing various personnel and other aircraft, to fall in the sea ahead of the ship with a big splash. Naturally it was assumed by all that I had failed to make my weapons switches safe and had fired it off by mistake. Luckily the film taken from Flyco, when developed, proved otherwise and I was exonerated.

Recovery to the ship was always a fairly stressful business. First of all you had to find the ship, which was not always where she said she was. You then joined the 'low wait' to await your 'Charlie time', the time you had to arrive on the deck. When called in to 'slot' you joined the circuit, having dumped fuel if necessary to get down to landing weight. The circuit was flown at 600 feet, turning in abeam the ship. You aimed to achieve your final approach speed/angle of attack about half way round the final turn. It was important not to line up on the ship's wake, which always gave a powerful visual distraction. You also had to cope with the funnel smoke, which sometimes was quite thick. The final part of the approach was flown at a constant speed/angle of attack, lined up exactly on the flight deck centre line and using the projector sight for glideslope. It was vital to concentrate utterly on the sight and the centre line, ignoring the rest of the ship's structure. There was no attempt to cushion the landing at all; the aircraft arrived at a fairly high rate of descent. You knew immediately if you had caught a wire because of the very rapid deceleration. In this case you throttled back immediately, so that the aircraft would be pulled back a short distance at the end of its roll out, thereby allowing the wire to fall clear of the arrestor hook.

Flight deck handlers would move out onto the flight deck as soon as they saw that you had caught a wire, in order to give the signals for taxiing clear as quickly as possible, as there was usually another aircraft 30–40 seconds behind you. The wire needed to be reset and checked before the next aircraft could land – this was done by a man wearing a large glove, which he ran down the length of the wire to check for any broken strands. If any were found that wire would not be reset. It was not uncommon for a recovery to start with all four wires available and to finish with only one.

Meanwhile, you taxied clear as fast as possible, folding the aircraft wings as you went, to be parked towards the bow of the ship. If no deceleration was felt on touchdown you immediately applied full power to go round, accompanied by a shower of red flares and the cry of 'Bolter, bolter' from Flyco. You then rejoined the circuit for another go. Once the ship and her squadrons were fully worked up you would often find the ship still turning onto her designated flying course as you 'slotted', only steadying on the correct course as the first aircraft rolled out on final approach. The desired landing interval by day was 30 seconds. In the event of poor weather a radar approach was used, similar to that on an airfield but without any glideslope information.

For most of my time on board, the Buccaneer was not cleared to fly at night from the ship because of problems associated with the 'hands off' launch technique. Eventually these difficulties were resolved and a full flight clearance was issued. Night flying was much more demanding. The catapult launch was very disorientating, as you were fired off into the dark without any visual references. Night recoveries were always radar approaches, irrespective of the weather. You looked up at 1 mile/300 feet, to see a very dimly lit flight deck. The projector sight was, however, very bright and the centre line was marked by a line of red lights that continued down vertically over the stern, thereby giving a very powerful indication if you were off centre line – this was known as 'the donkey's plonk'. Day flying from the deck was very exhilarating and I soon came to enjoy its challenge, but nobody really enjoyed night flying off the deck very much.

During my time embarked the ship stayed east of Suez, operating mainly in the Far East. We visited Hong Kong, Subic Bay and Singapore regularly. The ship was getting old by this time and generally seemed to suffer some form of mechanical breakdown on an almost weekly basis, requiring repair work to be done in a major dockyard. During one of these visits to Singapore a group of squadron aircrew drove an ancient minibus up to Thailand on an expedition. Thailand was un-discovered by western tourists at that time and I have memories of a country still very much stuck in the nineteenth century. The railway engines were all powered by steam, using wood for the boiler fires; they were all made in Glasgow in about 1900. I also recall taking another group of squadron ratings on a snorkelling expedition to a Malayan offshore island. We were delivered there by an ancient leaky fishing boat and left to our own devices for three days. There was no one else there. We camped on the beach; it was like a scene from Robinson Crusoe.

In May 1967 it was time for the ship to return to the UK for a major refit. We sailed up the west coast of Malaya (flying all the time) then crossed the Indian Ocean heading towards Aden. The British were in the process of withdrawing from Aden at this time and the security situation in the colony was very tense. There had been numerous terrorist acts and the prospect of a bloodbath during withdrawal was very real. On arrival off Aden the heat was intense and the ship's air conditioning system, never very efficient, failed completely. The ship's engineers decided to flood the flight deck in an attempt to cool down the ship's interior. The only effect this had was to produce incred-ibly hot fog below decks. We all went ashore to find some relief and were entertained in the Officers' Mess, RAF Khormaksar, our bus being guarded by soldiers with loaded machine-guns.

Also in Aden at the time was HMS *Hermes*, the carrier that was to take over our role east of Suez. Thus there was a rare opportunity for two Royal Navy aircraft carriers to operate together for a short time. We spent three or four days flying around the Aden Protectorate, accompanied by the Hunters from Khormaksar, in a display of airpower that was designed to impress upon the locals our capability to quell any unrest. This culminated in an enormous, unwieldy fifty-five aircraft flypast, consisting of all the serviceable Sea Vixens and Buccaneers from *Victorious* and *Hermes*, together with a large number of Hunters. The Hunters, who were all at the back of this huge gaggle, had a very difficult time staying in position.

We flew round Aden three times then split up to recover to our own aircraft carriers. Not wishing to be outdone, the 'fish heads' down below had taken advantage of this rare opportunity to operate two carriers in close company. They ended up with the two ships in line abreast, some two miles apart, both steaming into wind (what there was of it) to recover their aircraft. Unfortunately, they had put *Hermes*, which had a less angled deck, to the right of *Victorious*. This meant that to put the relative wind down her angled deck she had to steam on a heading that had her steadily closing with *Victorious*. Thus the two carriers got closer and closer and their individual landing patterns began to get completely intertwined, with confusing consequences. It was rumoured afterwards that somebody actually landed on the wrong ship without realising it, only to be rapidly fired off again.

We bade farewell to *Hermes* and steamed up the Red Sea toward the Suez Canal, with canvas swimming baths rigged on the flight deck to cool off in, uncertain as to whether or not we would be able to transit through the canal. The Middle East was in turmoil, with the prospect of a war between Israel and the Arab nations becoming more likely every day. We listened to the BBC World Service with great interest; the alternative route would have been all the way round South Africa. Nevertheless, we did go through the canal, but there were signs of military activity building up on both sides. We watched Egyptian Air Force pilots, who watched us from the bank, as we slowly sailed through. In the Great Bitter Lakes we passed the liner *Oriana*, which caused great excitement because of the large number of young, enthusiastic female passengers. Eventually *Victorious* emerged into the Mediterranean and we all prepared to disembark to the UK after a fast passage towards Gibraltar.

Just twelve hours before launching everything changed. We

perfect aircraft for a first solo.

Old cars were an essential feature of a Flight Cadet's lifestyle. My 1930 Morris Cowley with the boys aboard.

JP4 formation, Cranwell, 1963.

Gnat T1 line at Valley, 1964. An
exciting aircraft for student and
instructor.

Canberra B(I)8 with conventional
weapons.

Formation aeros over Anglesey.

16 Sqn Canberra, with USAF F105s, overflying Laarbruch QRA compound.

Paris take off, Kuantan, author in No 2 position.

Officer's accommodation, Kuantan, after regular evening storm.

The Canberra's conventional weapons load was rather small for such a large aircraft.

My Buccaneer course colleagues, RNAS Lossiemouth, 1966.

Hunter T8B, the dual control trainer for the Buccaneer.

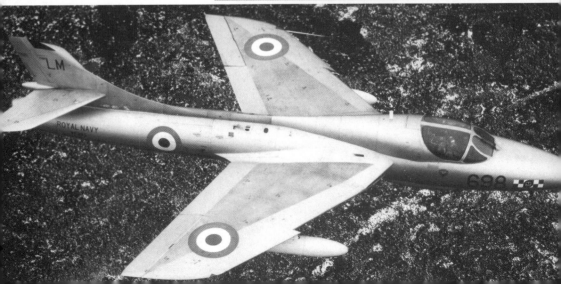

gaggle of early production Buccaneer S2s.

MS *Victorious*, leaving Portsmouth.

The Buccaneer had a far greater range of weapons than the Canberra.

Safely airborne from *Victorious*'s port catapult.

Final approach to 'Vic', as recorded by forward facing F95 camera in Buccaneer's photo-recce pack.

Buccaneer takes a wire.

I lose a Bullpup missile whilst landing on, April 1967.

Buccaneer firing 2″ rockets, Tain Range.

9 of 801's Buccaneers airborne.

ejection seat, showing the underwater assisted escape bladders inflated

ABOVE "... ISAAC NEWTON'S FIRST LAW ..."

BELOW " THANK YOU SIR JAMES ... FOR THE REST OF MY LIFE. "

PH
OF

A dramatic end to a 'Fam1' sortie, my student and I ejected successfully.

A 12 Squadron Buccaneer. This was my personal aircraft on 801 Sqn, now in service with the RAF.

Air to air refuelling
with 12 Sqn.

Recieving my Queen's
Commendation for
Valuable Services in the
Air from the Squadron
and Station Commanders.

...ots of 79 Sqn, RAF Brawdy, 1976. Author seated behind cockpit.

...nter of 79 Sqn over Soviet warship, Gibraltar, 1976.

3 Buccaneers of 237 OCU, RAF Honington, 1977.

The 'Silver Wings' flypast, June 1977. No sign of the chaos about to occur.

Taking command of 237 OCU, 1984.

Sidewinder firings at Aberporth, 1987.

were to stay in the Med for the time being, operating close to Malta, practising rocket attacks on our splash target and air-to-air refuelling, mainly for the Sea Vixens. No one knew at junior officer level what we might be expected to do if fighting was to break out between Israel and the Arab nations, an event that seemed more likely every day.

Unfortunately there was no Fleet Auxiliary tanker with aviation fuel in the Med, so on the morning of Monday 5 June we steamed into Grand Harbour, Valetta, to off-load a broken Sea Vixen and top up with aviation fuel. We had originally been told we would be remaining in harbour for two days' rest and recreation and a big formal cocktail party had been arranged for the first night at anchor, with the inevitable run ashore after-wards. There was also, as I recall, a rival party ashore, to be given by the local nurses and school teachers. We bachelors all planned to go to the latter event, as it offered much better possi-bilities after a long stretch afloat.

That morning, as the ship entered harbour, we listened on the Wardroom's radio to the news of the outbreak of hostilities between Israel, Egypt, Jordan and Syria. That evening, as we were all changing into shore rig for the schoolie/nurses' party, there came a pipe over the ship's public address system, announcing that all shore leave was cancelled, but that pre-planned shipboard events would continue. We all changed out of shore rig into cock-tail party uniform, when another pipe came, announcing that all shipboard events were now cancelled and that the ship would be sailing at 2200 hrs, etc, etc, with all the going-to-sea routine being trotted out. Groaning, we went back to our cabins to change into normal uniform for supper, when another pipe announced that all previous instructions were cancelled, shore leave was on again, the ship would not be sailing, etc, etc! All this took place in the space of twenty minutes or so.

And so we stayed in Malta for the whole of the seven-day war, doing nothing more aggressive than getting drunk at various parties ashore, whilst being accused by the Arab press of actively assisting the Israelis. Once the war was over we set sail, and a day later we were all launched off to fly back to Lossiemouth via Boscombe Down, where the aircraft were all searched thoroughly by Customs. I flew back in Buccaneer S2 XN 981, with our indefatigable junior engineer, Chris Esplin-Jones (Split Pin) in the back. We suffered a total pressurisation failure and had no hot air in the cockpit, so it was a very un-comfortable transit across France, followed by a long wait over Boscombe for the mist and ice in the cockpit to clear sufficiently to be able to land. Sadly, as events turned out, that was the end of my embarked flying, although I was not to know it at the time.

HMS *Victorious* arrived at Portsmouth about a week later and I went back on board to collect my bits and pieces. The ship was to stay in dock for a short refit before sailing again on her last commission. Whilst this was taking place 801 Squadron remained shore-based at Lossiemouth. We exchanged some of our aircraft for newer ones painted in the new overall grey paint scheme and carried on flying, waiting for the ship to put to sea again in November. The squadron provided an impressive fire-power demonstration for Exercise *Unison*, when three aircraft dropped their eight 1000-lb HE (high explosive) bombs in shallow dive attacks on Salisbury Plain, in front of a large group of Very Senior Officers. On the weekend before *Victorious* was due to leave the dry dock a fire broke out on 2 Deck when a water-boiling urn shorted out. The ship's fire main was not connected up as the ship was in the dry dock, so by the time the fire was extinguished by the dockyard fire brigade one sailor had died and some serious damage had been done, mainly to the wiring and cable looms. A week later the MoD announced that the ship would not put to sea again because the damage was considered too severe to justify the cost of repair. The Commissioning Party was turned into a Wake and even our farewell flypast of nine Buccaneers was frustrated by bad weather.

I remained with 801 Squadron throughout that winter and spring. The squadron remained at Lossiemouth and continued with operational flying activities, including the first air-to-air refuelling from Victor tankers. I also dropped a number of simu-lated napalm stores, called firebombs, on Tain Range. However, I do not believe that a real firebomb was ever released for actual service.

In April 1968 the squadron, now allocated to HMS *Hermes*, deployed to RAF El Adem, in Libya, for a major exercise. Our sister squadron, 893 Naval Air Squadron, flying Sea Vixens, deployed to Cyprus as defenders. We attacked Cyprus from El Adem on a regular basis, to be intercepted by Sea Vixens – it became very routine. The second half of the exercise was spent doing forward air control work in the desert with the army, which was much more fun.

It was just about this time that the Government announced that the RAF would be receiving Buccaneers as a long-awaited replacement for the Canberra, after many other projects had fallen by the wayside.

On return to Lossiemouth after the exercise in Libya, 801 Squadron was to reduce in size to a six-aircraft squadron in order to fit into the smaller *Hermes*. This meant a corresponding reduction in the number of aircrew so my time with the Fleet Air Arm was coming to an end. I flew back from El Adem in XT 269, expecting to have a non-stop transit refuelled *en route* by Victors. Unfortunately the cabin heating failed and the prospect of a six-hour transit at 30,000 feet in sub-zero temperatures was not appealing so we diverted into Malta.

Once on the ground Trevor Ling, my observer, fired up the HF radio and spoke to Lossiemouth explaining our predicament. An engineer was brought to the radio at Lossiemouth and gave instructions on how to fix the problem. I borrowed some tools from the RAF engineers and was busily pulling bits out of the Buccaneer when a group of RAF officers came over to have a look at their 'new' strike aircraft. They were not terribly impressed at what Trevor and I were doing to it!

Once back at Lossiemouth I discovered I was to go on a Qualified Flying Instructor's course at the Central Flying School, RAF Little Rissington. So I packed my bags and said farewell to the Royal Navy, not expecting to go back to them again but having had a wonderful two years with some of the best flying of my life. Embarked flying really was the most demanding aviation experience I have had, so I left sadly, not knowing what the future held.

CHAPTER SIX

Learning to Teach
– 1968 to 1969

RAF Little Rissington was the home of the Central Flying School (CFS) and a far cry from the front-line Fleet Air Arm. Neat rows of Jet Provosts, Chipmunks and Varsities were lined up on the flight line. Everything was very prim and proper. The Officers' Mess was a vast building with rows and rows of photographs of previous QFI courses along its corridors. Luckily my course had a large number of kindred spirits who had reluctantly been extracted from the front line, so the prospects for a robust social life were pretty good. Little Rissington was in the heart of the Cotswolds, with Bourton on the Water just down the hill with its many excellent pubs; Cheltenham was only a twenty-minute drive away.

We spent the first few weeks in the ground school learning about aerodynamics, meteorology, flight instruments, flight planning and instructional technique, all rather tedious and uninspiring. We then started flying the Jet Provost and after being checked out began to be taught the art of basic flying instruction. This consisted of being 'given' a typical flying lesson, such as 'effects of controls', by a staff QFI. Then you would practise the 'patter' with a course colleague, then finally 'give it back' to the staff QFI, who then 'gave' you another exercise. Needless to say, the mutual practice sorties did not consist of too much patter, but they were an excellent opportunity to practise advanced and convoluted aerobatics with one of your mates.

After some 30 hours and an initial handling check, the course was split up, the majority remaining on the Jet Provost and destined for the basic Flying Training Schools at Cranwell, Linton-on-Ouse, Church Fenton, Leeming, Acklington and Syerston. A few went on to the Chipmunk, which was flown by the University Air Squadrons – a very popular posting. A similarly small number went on to the Varsity for multi-engine instruction and only four went on to the Gnat, the advanced fast jet trainer. Just before I arrived at CFS it was hinted that I would be returning to the Buccaneer as a QFI after the course; I was therefore delighted to find myself on the Gnat course with one other RAF colleague and two naval officers.

The Gnat course was completely different from the Jet Provost element of the CFS course. For a start, the flying was undertaken at Kemble instead of from Little Rissington, as the runway at Little Rissington was considered too short for safe Gnat operations. This entailed a journey by ancient minibus every morning, which took about an hour, just about long enough to recover from the previous night's socialising.

The minibus was driven by an equally ancient civilian driver called Charlie. He would spend the entire journey telling us how he had never had an accident in all the years he had driven for the RAF. After many weeks of this torture we were all delighted when one day a wheel fell off the minibus as we descended the hill towards Bourton on the Water. Charlie burst into tears and took no further part in the proceedings. After recovering the wheel from the neighbouring field we escorted Charlie down the road to the Old New Inn in Bourton, where we sought assistance in the form of a restorative drink. Notwithstanding the early hour of the day, the landlord obligingly opened up, thereby putting any prospect of flying out of court, as he insisted that all of us should have a restorative brandy in view of the shock we had experienced. The party developed from then on and we didn't get back to Little Rissington until very late in the day!

Kemble was a sleepy hollow of an airfield deep in the Gloucestershire countryside. The CFS Gnat squadron shared

the accommodation with the Red Arrows who were flying the
Gnat at this time. The course itself was much more relaxed and
practical than what went on up at Little Rissington.

The rear seat of the Gnat was a very difficult seat to teach
from; the view ahead was minimal and many of the controls and
instruments in the back were different from the front. Teaching
from the back of a Gnat was a specialised art and it was difficult
to imagine what it would be like trying to teach a 'real' student,
rather than one of your course colleagues or one of the staff
instructors. We spent a lot of time transiting to and fro from RAF
Valley, either to take advantage of better weather, to use the
simulator, or to borrow other aircraft as the Gnat was
notoriously unserviceable.

Even walking out to the aircraft could be hazardous. The Red
Arrows also flew from Kemble and during the winter months
they had little to do – there was no formal work up programme
as today. Various team members would come to Kemble and get
airborne, float around the circuit until a couple of CFS students
began to walk out to their aircraft, and then attempt to blow
them over by flying down the flight line as low and fast as
possible.

Eventually, by late November 1968 the course was complete
and we were all signed up as B2 Qualified Flying Instructors,
instructors under probation as we had yet to be exposed to real
students. The end of course final guest night was a riotous affair
and included participation by live chickens and Morris dancers.
The Commandant, Air Commodore Ivor Broom, a wartime pilot
of great distinction, joined in the revelry with tremendous gusto.
The end of course photo was taken the next morning and was
not a pretty sight.

By now my ultimate destination as a QFI back at Lossiemouth
on the Buccaneer had been confirmed, but before that occurred I
was to go to No. 4 Flying Training School at RAF Valley to gain
some instructional experience. Valley had not changed much
since I had done my flying training there four years previously.
In the winter it was still wet and windy. The only difference was
that there was now a squadron of Hunters established to
provide additional training capacity, particularly for foreign
students, as the Gnat's high level of unserviceability made it
very difficult to achieve the training task. I joined the Refresher
Flight of 2 Squadron, which spent its time refreshing students

who had already passed the course and who were waiting for subsequent courses, so most of them were pretty competent. This did not really expose me to a genuine student who needed to be taught a new skill, but nevertheless it was a useful experience.

The Gnat continued to suffer from technical problems. On one occasion I was up at Lossiemouth on a land-away navigation exercise; after getting airborne I was instructed to land as soon as possible using minimum control inputs. It subsequently transpired that another aircraft's aileron control cables had snapped in flight so all Gnats were immediately grounded for inspection and repair. After two days of hanging around in a sweaty immersion suit I got fed up and went back to Valley by train, still wearing my immersion suit and clutching my flying helmet. I was a source of constant amusement and inquiry from all the other train passengers on what proved to be a very slow journey.

By the end of April 1969 it was time to move on again, this time back to RNAS Lossiemouth and 736 Naval Air Squadron. I was to be a member of the RAF team of instructors, all of whom had flown the Buccaneer with the Fleet Air Arm. We were to assist in training the first eight courses of RAF aircrew destined to fly the Buccaneer.

CHAPTER SEVEN

Teaching on the Buccaneer – 1969 to 1972

After a long drive from Anglesey to the north of Scotland I arrived back at Lossiemouth late on a Saturday night, expecting to go straight to bed in a deserted Wardroom Mess. I found the mother and father of all parties going on – HMS *Eagle* was in the Moray Firth and many of her crew had gone ashore for the day. When it was time for them to go back on board, a strong wind prevented the ship's boats from running a shuttle service so they were all stuck at Lossiemouth for the night. There was no accommodation and the party was going at full throttle. At some point in the early hours of the morning the Wardroom piano was reduced to its component parts, then very cleverly reconstructed. Next day, during lunchtime drinks after the church service, a senior officer placed his glass of gin and tonic on the piano – it collapsed spectacularly. By this time the perpetrators were all back on board *Eagle* and untouchable.

I joined 736 Naval Air Squadron with two other pilots (Tim Cockerell and Jerry Yates) and three navigators (Barry Dove, Mick Whybro and Dave Laskey) who had all served on Navy Buccaneer squadrons. We were the team responsible for training the first eight courses of RAF aircrew, although in practice we were completely integrated with the naval aircrew on the squadron; we flew equally with RN and RAF students.

Additionally there were about fifty RAF ground crew attached to 736 Naval Air Squadron, commanded by a flight lieutenant engineer officer, John Harvey. Their role was to learn about the aircraft and assist with the maintenance task. Eight old and rather tired Buccaneer S1s were taken out of storage, maintained by the RAF and used for all the RAF flying tasks as there were insufficient numbers of S2s to meet the extra flying generated by the unexpected addition of the RAF training.

My first task was to refresh and qualify as a QFI on the Hunter, our only dual control aircraft, which was used for all early handling sorties and instrument flying. Our Hunters had the Buccaneer's flight instrument system installed on the left-hand side for the student pilot. That apart, it shared no common handling characteristics with the Buccaneer and was much easier to fly. I also became an Instrument Rating Instructor (IRI), which involved a pleasant two-week detachment at RNAS Yeovilton to fly with the Naval Flying Standards Flight. Next, it was time to become checked out as a QFI on the Buccaneer.

The Buccaneer QFI sat in the back seat, devoid of any flying controls and with minimal flight instruments to assist him. The view forward was quite good, especially on the right-hand side, as the seat was higher and off set to the right compared with the front seat. Thus you could monitor the progress of the sortie quite effectively, and provide advice, encouragement and remonstrations to the tyro pilot in the front, but there was no way of controlling the aircraft.

The tyro pilot would complete at least six simulator rides, culminating in a complex emergencies sortie, and three trips in the Hunter. These three trips were very useful in that they gave the QFI a fair idea of his student's ability and competence. Then it was time for the Fam 1, the student's first Buccaneer sortie and also his first solo. Some of these sorties were nerve-racking events for both individuals. The sortie profile included a climb to height for some handling at around 30,000 feet with and without auto stabilisation, a maximum rate descent to 10,000 feet for more handling and basic aerobatics, a descent to low level for a high-speed run, then some practice at flying the aircraft in the landing configuration. Then it was back to the airfield for a long straight-in approach, followed by visual circuits, culminating hopefully in a successful landing. If a major unserviceability occurred at a critical stage in the sortie, such as an engine failure on take-off or in the circuit, the chances of a successful outcome were remote and totally dependent on the reactions of the student pilot. The S1 version of the Buccaneer was particularly underpowered and not very serviceable so every Fam 1 was an exciting event. Thereafter the QFI did not fly in the back again, handing over to an experienced staff observer/navigator, unless an individual was having particular difficulties on the early sorties.

Apart from Fam 1, the rest of the flying on 736 Naval Air Squadron was fairly routine and typical of an operational conversion outfit. There were still quite a few RN aircrew going through and they enjoyed a longer and more comprehensive course than their RAF colleagues, including air-to-air refuelling, visual and photo recce and DLP. Having experienced an enjoyable tour with the Navy I often felt my loyalty being pulled in two directions; the Navy were faced with a steady run down of its fixed wing activities, which were being taken over by the RAF and they were most unhappy about this. I had much sympathy with them. Relationships remained cordial throughout between RN and RAF staff on 736 Naval Air Squadron, because of our shared experience of carrier operations, but there were many occasions when RAF students got the cold shoulder treatment. John Harvey and his engineers performed marvels in keeping the elderly and unloved S1s going, especially as none of the troops were allowed to live at Lossiemouth and had to commute daily from Kinloss.

Socially the life at Lossiemouth was as good as ever, there were many living in the Wardroom and there was much to do in that remote part of Scotland. I kept a small boat in Hopeman harbour, some five miles down the coast, and sailed it regularly down the Great Glen each summer. The Inchnacardoch Hotel in Fort Augustus was a regular haunt, being run by an ex-Fleet Air Arm pilot, Bill MacDonald, who had a large family of daughters. I was best man to Andy Evans, a navigator who had been with the RN and who married one of the daughters. I spent many happy weekends exploring the far north of Scotland, sailing and skiing in the winter at Aviemore.

The two years of RAF training passed very quickly and generally without major incidents. By December 1970 the last RAF course had arrived so the end of my association with the Fleet Air Arm was in sight. The main RAF base for the Buccaneer force was at Honington in Suffolk, with further squadrons planned to form at Laarbruch, so all of the RAF staff expected to move on to one or other of these bases.

On 1 December I was scheduled to fly with Flying Officer Ivor Evans on his Fam 1. By this time the S1s were getting decidedly tired. Their Gyron Junior engines, never known for their user-friendly handling characteristics, were extremely difficult to accelerate in a crosswind on the runway. You often had to point directly into wind, brakes on, to persuade the engines to accelerate up to full power, then turn to line up with the runway as you started the take-off roll. The aircraft's acceleration was so sluggish that this evolution never presented any difficulty.

Ominously, on this Fam 1 we had great difficulty getting the port engine to accelerate through the inlet guide vane range before take-off but, with persistence, it finally wound up and off we went. All went well until we returned to the circuit. We ended up too high and close on the first circuit so, at 200 feet, I told Ivor to overshoot and go round again. When he pushed the throttles forward for full power all we got from the port engine was a lot of loud bangs and choking noises and no thrust. With commendable alacrity for a pilot on his first flight on type, Ivor lifted the wheels and got the airbrake in, but with the landing flap down and the blown ailerons and tailplane bleeding large amounts of air from the one good engine, Isaac Newton's First Law soon kicked in. It very rapidly became evident that this sortie was not going to end satisfactorily without the help of Martin-Baker's rocket-assisted deck chair. I had loosened my shoulder harness to see ahead, round the top of Ivor's ejection seat and this was no time to start tightening straps. Shouting EJECT, EJECT, I pulled the firing handle between my legs, and after a big bang I was looking down through my feet at the airfield grass coming up fast. I arrived on terra firma like a sack of spuds thrown from a second floor window.

After establishing that I was alive and that my back hurt, my next priority was to get my SARBE (Search and Rescue Beacon Equipment) going to qualify for the silver tankard that Burndept Electronics (the manufacturers) gave to all aircrew who used their excellent product in a rescue. When an asbestos-suited fireman appeared in my field of vision I told him rudely to go away as I still hadn't got the beacon working yet. Given that I was sprawled in the middle of Lossiemouth airfield he clearly thought I was delirious, took it gently from me and made soothing noises until the ambulance arrived. Ivor also jumped out successfully.

The hapless Buccaneer flopped on the airfield, narrowly missing some people mending a radar aerial, and slithered to a halt on its belly; the cockpit section broke off and a fire started. The big fire tender, when it finally arrived after getting bogged down in the grass, squirted foam all over it trying to extinguish the fire and shut down the starboard engine, which perversely continued running at full power for a while. A putrid smell drifted away on the wind and gave rise to serious complaints from lunchtime drinkers in the Wardroom. I spent an uncomfortable three weeks lying flat on my back in Dr Gray's Hospital, getting my vertebrae back in place, drinking smuggled whisky and annoying the nurses. Ivor, whose straps were tight, was back flying in a couple of days.

A few years later, by now a married and more responsible officer altogether, I visited the Martin-Baker factory and met that great man Sir James Martin. I think I speak for every ejectee when I say thank you, Sir James, and all at Martin-Baker, for the rest of my life.

Barely a week after my accident, a Buccaneer S1 being flown by two RAF students suffered a massive uncontained engine failure shortly after take-off. The pilot ejected successfully but tragically the navigator was killed because a piece of Perspex from the shattered canopy jammed the ejection seat's release mechanism and he was unable to separate himself from the seat in time. This accident brought Buccaneer S1 flying to a halt for ever. Some of the remaining airframes were delivered to other airfields for use as Gate Guards or for battle damage repair work, the rest went to museums or scrap. I spent the rest of the winter at Lossiemouth recuperating then finally had to leave in March 1971 to continue my instructional duties at the newly formed Buccaneer Operational Conversion Unit, No. 237, based at RAF Honington in Suffolk. I returned to full flying duties after a minor argument with the Station Medical Officer, who insisted that I would be grounded for a year; happily the back specialist at the hospital at Ely overrode his decision.

*   *   *

RAF Honington was a typical pre-war bomber base set in the Suffolk countryside. It had been closed for a few years before reopening for the RAF's Buccaneer squadrons in 1969. There was only one squadron resident, 12 Squadron, so it was a bit of a sleepy hollow compared with Lossiemouth. Setting up 237 OCU was quite a challenge. I recall having to visit the scrap heap at the recently closed down RAF Stradishall to recover briefing boards for our briefing rooms as Honington seemed unable to provide any. We opened for business in June 1971 and the pattern of activity was almost identical to what had taken place at Lossiemouth. Unfortunately there was no flight simulator at Honington so many journeys were made up north to use the simulator that was still in use at Lossiemouth.

Our early students were a complete mixture, ranging from first tourists with no previous experience through to our future Station Commander and even the Air Officer Commanding. The RAF looked on the Buccaneer as a sort of mini V bomber and much to our horror tried to make us operate it in a similar fashion to a V bomber. Not surprisingly we resisted as we saw the Buccaneer as more of a larger Hunter fighter-bomber. Luckily for us, our new Station Commander, Group Captain Peter Bairsto, known to all as 'the Bear', agreed with the maxi Hunter philosophy and fought hard for this in the corridors of power. The OCU was commanded by an extremely handsome and upper class Wing Commander, Anthony Fraser; his senior flight commander and Chief Flying Instructor (CFI), Squadron Leader David Mulinder, was a man of great character and wit. We soon settled into the business of training RAF aircrew on the Buccaneer and it was not long before some RN aircrew started to appear on the instructional staff.

One night one of the first tour student navigators, David Herriot, and I were programmed to fly in a three-aircraft formation; we were to be the lead aircraft. Unusually it was a busy night at Honington, with a number of visiting aircraft including a twin-engined Andover passenger aircraft that was bringing in a load of visiting VIPs. It was also a very dark night without moonlight or stars.

All went well with the sortie up to the point when I lined up on the runway as a three-aircraft formation for a 30-second stream take-off. I should point out that the Buccaneer, because of its naval ancestry, was not at that time equipped with a landing lamp, as they are superfluous on aircraft carriers. It was therefore not possible to see anything in the darkness ahead apart from the runway edge lighting.

Brakes off, full power and off we went. Initially all seemed OK. The airspeed indicator began to give readings but, at about 100 knots, the aircraft rapidly decelerated and came to a halt. I still had full power applied and thought at first I had inadvertently put the arrestor hook down but, no, the selector was in the up position and there was no green light showing it to be down. Luckily none of the aircraft behind had started their take-off roll so I called Air Traffic Control with a message that I 'seem to have become stuck on the runway,' or words to that effect. Air Traffic Control naturally assumed that I had inadvertently put the hook down and had engaged the approach end arrestor cable – this had happened before. Doubtless thinking what idiots we were – you could tell from the tone of their voices – they sent a vehicle out to have a look at us. By this time I had throttled back to await developments.

The vehicle approached, stopped a short distance away, then rapidly reversed away. Air Traffic Control, now in a completely different tone of voice, told us to shut down but not to unstrap or attempt to get out until outside help had arrived. Eventually a team appeared from the darkness with an extending set of steps, which they gingerly placed by the cockpit. They then signalled us, from a distance, to get out. When we climbed down we saw that the arrestor cable was wrapped around the nose-wheel leg. The whole thing was stretched tight like some giant catapult; it appeared to be about to launch our Buccaneer, backwards, down the runway towards the rest of the formation who were still patiently sitting there.

By now the Bear, who was not noted for tolerance of professional foul-ups, had arrived on the scene. Breathing fire from his nostrils he demanded to know precisely who was to blame for this shambles that had closed his airfield in such a thoughtless fashion, and in the middle of a VIP visit! Of course in the darkness of the night no one had a clue as to how this had happened or how to extract the aircraft from its imminent backwards launch. As the debate and argument continued amongst all parties out there on the runway, the finger of suspicion seemed to be pointing more and more at my student and me. In the hubbub we both agreed it would be safer to make ourselves scarce and to slip away to the bar.

The answer to this saga only became clear the next morning. Lying on the grass beside the runway was found the shattered remains of a metal stand that the fire crews used to hold up the arrestor cable about 3 feet above the runway, to allow them to move the rubber grommets that supported the cable more easily into position. Whilst re-rigging the cable after the arrival of the VIP's Andover the night before, they were hassled by Air Traffic Control to hurry up as my formation was already taxiing. In their haste to get the job done they forgot to remove the stand. I then hit it on take-off and inevitably collected the cable around the nosewheel leg. Amazingly there was little damage to the Buccaneer; it needed a new nosewheel leg and two new under-wing tanks, but that was all. Not long afterwards all RAF Buccaneers were equipped with a landing lamp but whether or not this would have influenced the outcome is impossible to say.

During the autumn of 1971 a change in the rules and regulations allowed single officers to live off base in their own accommodation so Peter Bucke, Peter Huett and I found a pad in the depths of Suffolk, which we started to rent. This move off base caused consternation in the upper echelons of the command structure at Honington but the Bear was told there was nothing he could do to stop it. Hearing of his discomfiture at this turn of events we decided, out of devilment, to invite him to our house-warming party. Imagine our amazement when he accepted! As the day approached we were informed that, unfortunately, he had been summoned to a conference at Strike Command headquarters but that he would send a couple of representatives to stand in for him. These turned out to be his daughter and a friend of hers, Julia Bennett, who lived locally. We were to pick them both up in a local pub, The Dog in Norton, and they would be escorted by another, more suitable, bachelor, Peter Gooding. So that is how I met my future wife, in a pub, being escorted by a man considered far more reliable than I! It was not long before Julia and I announced our engagement.

By the spring of 1972 all six of us who had been RAF instructors on 736 NAS and then 237 OCU had been instructing for three years continuously, so the RAF decided to split us up and send us on our various ways. Barry Dove went off to a ground tour at Bawtry, the Group headquarters; Jerry Yates was posted to

Germany and the newly re-formed 16 Squadron; Dave Laskey and Mick Whybro went off to various courses and Tim Cockerell and I were to go to 12 Squadron at Honington.

Events moved very quickly; my instructional tour ended the day before my wedding on 3 June 1972. Shortly before the wedding, the Duke of Windsor (Edward VIII) died and a period of official Court Mourning was declared. We were then informed by the protocol staffs that if uniform was to be worn at ceremonial events, such as weddings, the wearers would have to wear black arm bands. Thus it was that I, my best man Peter Huett, the Guard of Honour and all Service guests were clad in black armbands at my wedding. There were many remarks about whether this marked mourning for a lost era of bachelor excesses, as typified by the alleged damage caused to the Officers' Mess bar during my stag night!

CHAPTER EIGHT

No. 12 Squadron – 1972 to 1975

After a three-week honeymoon break in Corfu it was back to work with a vengeance, on a new squadron that was the sole RAF Buccaneer front-line squadron based in the UK. No. 12 Squadron (motto 'Leads the Field') had recently been taken over by a new squadron commander, Wing Commander Nigel Walpole, a man of great energy and vision who had recently been rushed through his operational conversion from a ground tour.

Whilst Julie and I were enjoying the delights of Corfu in the spring, 12 Squadron had suffered a fatal accident in which two aircrew lost their lives, one being the USAF exchange officer. The circumstances of the accident threw considerable doubt on the control and supervision of flying on the squadron, especially as the squadron commander had been a member of the fatal sortie's formation. Thus I arrived on a Monday morning to find the squadron in a state of considerable turmoil. It was not long before the news came that Nigel Walpole was to be relieved of his command and replaced by Wing Commander Ian Henderson, a flight commander who had recently left for a ground tour. He was given an instant promotion to acting rank and a rapid return to the cockpit. To say that squadron morale at this time was low is an understatement.

Nigel Walpole's send off was for me a grim event, as I was

Station Duty Officer and had to attempt damage limitation in the Mess, unfortunately not with much success since at the height of the evening's excesses someone invited the Bear over. He came and was not amused. His wrath was directed at me, his representative, the next Monday morning. There was only one thing to do; tell him politely that it had not been sensible for him to come and that if he had stayed away all the mess would have been cleared up without him knowing. After boiling over for a bit he calmed down and seemed to accept this response as fair. However, overall it was not a happy start to a new tour.

No. 12 Squadron's task was to provide a maritime strike/ attack capability for the Supreme Commander Atlantic (SACLANT); its secondary role was nuclear strike in support of the UK National Plan. Ian Henderson's task was to restore the squadron's morale and *esprit de corps*. He was also charged by the Bear to develop proper tactics for multi-aircraft formation attacks on surface ships, a skill that the squadron had never fully got to grips with since it re-formed as a Buccaneer squadron in 1969. There were a number of relatively new squadron members so we all set to with a will. It was hard work.

Looking in my logbook I see that I regularly flew 35 hours a month, a lot of it at night, with many detachments away from Honington. Within weeks of my arrival we were detached to Stornoway in the Hebrides, whilst Lossiemouth's main runway was repaired. It had been badly damaged by a Buccaneer that caught fire during take-off for the big autumn exercise that always took place in the North Sea and Atlantic. We soon found ourselves flying as far south as Gibraltar with the assistance of air-to-air refuelling. Stornoway was a very primitive forward operating base with minimal facilities but the locals were extremely hospitable. We lived in breeze-block huts in communal sleeping areas. There was a field kitchen and a large Mess tent that served as an Officers' Mess. There was a large hangar, which was empty of all facilities and full of seagull excrement. The runway was rather short so a portable arrestor gear was brought in to cater for emergencies. On Sundays we were confined to camp and no flying took place in respect of the strictly observed Sabbath in that part of the world.

During the detachment the Air Officer Commanding No. 1 Group, Air Vice Marshal Horsley, a distinguished wartime

Mosquito pilot, paid us a visit. On arrival he was taken to our Mess tent and given lunch. During the meal he described his sadness at discovering the previous evening that the family cat had been run over and squashed when let out for its evening tiddle. Suitably sympathetic noises and comments were made round the table.

The next item on the programme was a visit downtown to the Procurator Fiscal. The Air Marshal and the Bear travelled in a staff car, preceded by a Land Rover driven by the Stornoway Station Commander, a squadron leader. On reaching the edge of Stornoway a cat ran out in front of the convoy and . . . was squashed. 'Drive on' commanded the Bear. 'Stop!' shouted the Air Marshal. The party then disembarked from their vehicles and the corporal driver, holding the very dead cat by the tail, was instructed by the Air Marshal to find its owner and offer suitable sympathy and remuneration. However, none of the inhabitants of the houses in the immediate area would have anything to do with the dead cat, so, with time pressing, it was thrown over a wall and the convoy set forth again. The Procurator's hospitality with the whisky was generous and the Air Marshal became somewhat happier.

The next event was a fishing expedition leaving Stornoway harbour in a small motor boat that I had been detailed to oversee. Thus two very merry senior officers descended into the boat after leaving the Procurator's lodgings and we chugged out into Loch Stornoway. No fish were caught and as we turned for home at the furthest point from the harbour the engine died. Nothing would persuade it to start again so there was no other option but to row back, naturally against the tide. At least the Bear had the decency to help with the rowing but the Air Marshal sat glumly in the stern, the effects of the Procurator's whisky having worn off. Overall, it was a disastrous afternoon but most amusing to look back on.

Moreover, the disasters continued. At the Squadron Dining-in Night that evening one of the pilots, Rob Williams, foolishly promised to supply the Air Marshal with fresh lobsters the next morning for him to take back to Bawtry. Rob sadly had more to drink that night than he had anticipated and seriously overslept. He was woken from his camp bed next morning and summonsed to the Air Marshal's Hunter. Rob stood in the keening Hebridean gale, clad only in a Paisley pattern dressing gown and wearing red leather slippers, attempted to explain the lack of lobsters to the Air Marshal, who was already strapped in. We had no more VIP visits after that.

Planning the flying programme on 12 Squadron was originally rather a 'hit and miss' business, with one or other of the numerous squadron leaders getting the task at short notice. With the complications of booking activities well ahead, it was decided to give the programming task to two competent flight lieutenants as a full-time commitment. Thus Bruce Chapple and I became the 12 Squadron programming and planning team, a busy but rewarding task. It also meant that we could take advantage of the good deals when they came along, as long as we were not too obvious about it.

One of these was a BBC TV programme called 'Skywatch'. This was a programme featuring all RAF activities, including a firepower demonstration on Salisbury Plain. No. 12 Squadron's involvement was to provide four aircraft, each firing a full war load of 2-inch rockets with high-explosive heads. This amounted to 144 rockets per aircraft, something that none of us had ever done before. Normally we simply went to the range and fired nine rockets singly in an academic pattern; occasionally we would do a first run attack using an operational profile but merely firing a single rocket. Thus this exercise was a never to be repeated opportunity.

The target was a concrete tower about 20 feet high, surrounded by a group of redundant vehicles. We were told to take our time around the pattern and only fire when completely happy. When the moment came, it was astonishing. The whole of the area in front of the aircraft was obscured in smoke and rocket exhaust flame. There was a powerful stench of cordite in the cockpit and in spite of the fast ripple mode of fire being used it seemed to take for ever for all the rockets to leave their launcher pods. Subsequent viewing of the video of what happened in the target area, which of course we did not see from the cockpit, was awe-inspiring. The concrete tower, which for years had withstood efforts by army artillery to destroy it, crumbled and disappeared. The vehicles were smashed to pieces and hurled about all over the place. Our opinion of the 2-inch rocket, which up to this point had been rather disparaging, suddenly improved by a large amount!

The other weapons available to us were really no different from many years' previous. Our conventional bomb was the 1000-lb high-explosive bomb, which could be fitted with a retard or ballistic tail and air or ground burst fuses, and the 2-inch rocket described above. For night illumination we had the Lepus flare, which was tossed in a ballistic trajectory towards the target before deploying a parachute and igniting. Our conventional attack tactics had to be designed around these weapons. Thus we ended up with large formations of eight aircraft split into two sections of four. One section was responsible for defence suppression, using a toss attack to throw a large number of air burst bombs towards the target in the hope that radar gun laying and missile guidance systems would be knocked off line. The other section would then close for an accurate shallow dive, level retard or rocket attack to finish off the target.

Whether or not this would have worked out successfully for real was uncertain. We spent many hours in the air co-ordinating these attacks and on a good day they worked out well. On a bad day, with poor weather, aircraft snags and poor communications they could be a nightmare. Since they all involved getting very close to the target with no screening from the ship's defences, we all felt very vulnerable.

At night we reduced the aircraft numbers and used the Lepus flare to illuminate the target before carrying out a dive attack, which was quite scary on a dark night. On one occasion I did succeed in sinking the splash target being towed by a frigate, very much to both my and the ship's amazement. Of course we also had the ultimate, nuclear, option but again the delivery aircraft would have been very vulnerable.

During my tour on 12 Squadron some welcome new equipment began to appear. A much improved Radar Warning Receiver was fitted into the tailplane fairing, which, when combined with the old Wide-Band Homer, gave us a much better ability to detect and classify hostile radar transmissions. During 1973 we began to receive the Martel missile system. Martel was an acronym for Missile Anti Radar and Television. It was designed as a defence suppression weapon in its anti-radar mode and a ship sinker in its TV mode. It was quite big, about 12 feet long, and the Buccaneer could carry four anti-radar, three TV missiles or a combination of both. The anti-radar version could be launched from low level about 20 miles from the target. It would climb to height then dive supersonically on to the target, exploding close to any radar it was locked on to. The TV version was launched at low level about 12 miles from the target. The launch aircraft could then turn away and, through a data link pod, establish a TV and radio command link with the missile, which cruised at about 800 feet and 500 knots. The missile had a TV camera in its nose and the picture was displayed on a TV screen in the navigator's cockpit. The navigator could control the missile through a small control column and guide it with great accuracy into the target ship once it came in view. That, at least, was the theory. The TV missile was thus limited to daylight and reasonably good weather but, combined with its anti-radar version, it did at last gives us a reasonable stand-off attack capability.

We were involved in the trial firings in Aberporth Range off the Welsh coast. On one occasion it was decided to combine a Martel trial firing with a trial to test whether a Phantom's radar could pick up a missile like Martel, which was similar in size to a number of Soviet cruise missiles. There was a layer of cloud on the day from 1500 feet to 2500 feet so the Martel would be below this whilst the Phantom would be above. The missile was duly fired and set off towards the target; the Phantom was head on to it and cruising at 3000 feet. The Phantom's navigator soon locked on to the Martel. Unfortunately, as soon as the Buccaneer's navigator selected the terminal phase of the attack his TV screen went blank and he lost all control of his Martel. Shortly afterwards the Martel shot out of the cloud cover going vertically upwards, narrowly missing the Phantom on both its upward and subsequent downward trajectory. It was decided not to repeat this trial again!

Eventually, an American active electronic countermeasures pod began to appear, giving us the ability to jam hostile radars. By the mid-1970s, therefore, the Buccaneer was able to detect maritime threats, jam them, then carry out accurate stand-off attacks with missiles and close-in attacks with bombs and rockets.

Many of our detachments were to Malta, Gibraltar and Cyprus, mainly for various exercises with the Royal Navy. I participated in a firepower demonstration in Cyprus when the first public demonstration of the BL755 cluster bomb took place, delivered from a Buccaneer flown by the Bear.

Cyprus was invaded by the Turks in 1974; when this occurred I was on leave and for the first and only time in my career I was recalled from leave. I was one of the last to get back to Honington and the first four crews were already walking to their aircraft to set off for Cyprus when I got into the squadron late that evening. They never got airborne and we spent the next three days hanging around in expectation of going. Ultimately we were stood down and never went.

However, there was an amusing sequel to this. One of our aircraft was in Engineering Wing undergoing a minor servicing. The Engineering Wing staff, with commendable enthusiasm, worked day and night to get the aircraft serviceable quickly and it was soon delivered to the squadron. What we did not know was that the Engineering Wing staff had prepared it for an over-seas deployment 'by the book', which involved fitting in the bomb door a full set of aircraft access steps, intake blanks, ground locks and engineering manuals, a considerable load. We on the squadron were unaware of this load and as normally the bomb door was not rotated very often, so it remained inside but unknown. A few days later we were involved in a demonstra-tion to members of the Royal College of Defence Studies (very important people), who were embarked on a destroyer in the North Sea. After carrying out our demo co-ordinated attack we re-formed for a low fast flypast over the ship. The formation leader, the Boss, briefed that we should all open our bomb doors just as we approached the ship, as this action made a wonderful noise. Imagine my surprise when I saw his door open and the ladders, locks, intake blanks and manuals all fell out. Luckily, given their poor ballistic qualities, they fell into the sea well short of the destroyer but the Navy and College staff and students were equally astonished. I understand that there was a tense exchange of signals between the Royal Navy and RAF Honington on the incident.

After nearly three busy years with 12 Squadron the RAF's posting people caught up with me again and it was time to move on. For a short while a ground tour seemed possible and too awful to contemplate, but then commonsense prevailed and I was posted to the Tactical Weapons Unit, flying Hunters, based at RAF Brawdy far in the west of Wales.

In the New Year's Honours List of 1975 I was delighted to discover that I had been awarded a Queen's Commendation for Valuable Services in the Air, presumably for three years' of undetected crime. This was presented to me on the occasion of the Squadron's 70th Anniversary celebrations. So in March 1975 I left Honington, 12 Squadron and the Buccaneer for the wild west of Wales.

CHAPTER NINE

Hunters in Wales
– 1975 to 1976

RAF Brawdy was situated at the most westerly end of Pembrokeshire. Apart from a small section of Ireland, the next dry land was the eastern coast of the USA. Brawdy had been a Royal Naval Air Station but the Navy had withdrawn in 1972 leaving the airfield empty, apart from a secret US Navy facility, which was the terminal of a submarine listening system used to detect the passage of submarines transiting the North Atlantic. Thus there was an urgent need to reopen the airfield to full-time operations so that the US Navy facility could be properly supported. No. 229 OCU, happily based at RAF Chivenor in Devon and flying Hunters, eventually drew the short straw. Renamed the Tactical Weapons Unit (TWU), it reluctantly moved to Brawdy from Chivenor in October 1974.

Brawdy was a very different airfield to operate Hunters from compared with Chivenor. The weather was very unpredictable and difficult to forecast; the nearest diversion airfields, St Athan and Valley, were a long distance away and not always available; the only navigation aid was an old DME (Distance Measuring Equipment) beacon that rarely worked; the F6 and T7 Hunters were always short of fuel and the living accommodation was primitive by RAF standards. Nearly all the aircrew longed to be back at Chivenor in glorious Devon rather than be at this windswept outpost. Thus it was not the happiest of units that I arrived on after an incredibly long car journey from Honington one wet Sunday evening.

The TWU was divided into three squadrons, 63, 79 and 234, all having reserve status and strong traditions as fighter squadrons. There was a large fleet of Hunters consisting of T7s, F6s and FGA9s. There were also three Meteors for target towing and a couple of Jet Provosts for the Joint Forward Air Control Unit. The TWU's task was to provide tactical flying training and weaponry for pilots graduating from advanced flying training who were destined to move on to Harrier, Jaguar, Lightning, Buccaneer and Phantom Operational Conversion Units. It also provided short refresher courses for senior officers returning to flying duties and for newly arrived staff pilots; this job was done by 79 Squadron. The TWU's war role was to provide short-range day air defence for the main fighter bases of Leuchars, Binbrook, Coningsby and Wattisham; additionally a permanent detachment of three Hunters was maintained at Gibraltar to provide air defence for the Rock and to deter Spanish interference with inbound and outbound air traffic.

I joined 79 Squadron for the short conversion course. Initially this was not too challenging as I was already a current Hunter pilot. Things got more interesting when the weapons phase started and I was reintroduced to air-to-ground gunnery, much more effective with the Hunter's 30-mm Aden cannon than it had been with the old Canberra 20-mm Hispano. We also fired 68-mm SNEB rockets in shallow dive attacks, very similar to the Buccaneer's 2-inch rockets, and dropped practice bombs from shallow dives. This latter event was a purely academic routine, there being no real bomb in the RAF inventory that the Hunter could deliver. The delights of air combat were also experienced but sadly not air–to-air firing, which was reserved for long course students or senior officers going back to the air defence world.

At the end of the short course I was delighted to be posted to 79 Squadron as it certainly seemed to enjoy the best quality of life. Dealing with senior officers returning to flying appointments was an entertaining business. Most were excellent and enthusiastic pilots only too keen to scrub off the rust of a ground tour and get on with the flying but there were exceptions. Some of the American exchange officers had great difficulty in coping with what for them was a primitive aircraft, dreadful weather and a lack of understanding of RAF operating procedures and language. Some RAF pilots had been too long on the ground and didn't make it through the course and were returned to a less demanding environment.

When the weather was good the flying was superb, with the whole of Wales, Devon and Cornwall as our playground. Sorties in the F6 and T7 were always short of fuel; the Hunter's fuel gauges had the regrettable characteristic of over reading when flying fast at low level. The F6 and FGA9 had two bingo lights, directly connected to float switches, which illuminated at 650 lb a side and reset the gauges to the correct reading. This was always a disconcerting event, especially if it occurred in the middle of Wales during a bounced low-level simulated attack profile sortie. For some reason the T7 didn't have bingo lights, so T7 pilots lived in ignorance of their true fuel state. At least the FGA9, with its 230-gallon external tanks, had a bit of an advantage over the F6s and T7s with their 100-gallon external tanks.

Brawdy had two runways. One was quite a bit shorter than the other, and neither orientated into the prevailing westerly wind. The F6 had no brake parachute so could sometimes be challenging to stop. There was one memorable occasion when an F6 went into the barrier on the main runway, followed quickly by another going into the barrier on the secondary runway, leaving five Hunters still airborne and very short of fuel. They were told to divert to St Athan in poor weather, dropping their tanks in St Brides Bay on the way. Two aircraft never got there, ending up even further away at Cardiff by mistake, taxiing in on fumes.

We bombarded Pembrey Range ceaselessly, with practice bombs, rockets and 30-mm cannon. The weapons system in the Hunter was primitive and the vital switches to operate it seemed to differ between individual aircraft; thus a fair number of drop tanks also got dropped into Pembrey inadvertently. Air-to-air firing was conducted against a banner towed at 200 knots behind a Meteor or a Hunter. It was often said that if the Russians had attacked the UK using banners at 200 knots we would have slaughtered them, but high-speed aircraft targets would have been altogether much more challenging.

*   *   *

Despite its remoteness the county of Dyfed, or Pembrokeshire, as its inhabitants insisted on calling it, was a delightful area when it wasn't raining. The coastline was dramatic and there was a very English feel about the whole area. It was also known as Little England Beyond Wales. In the local village of Little Haven there was a superb pub, The Swan, run by an ex-79 Squadron World War Two pilot, George Nelson Edwards. The squadron naturally gravitated to this establishment. There were no Married Quarters at the airfield apart from the Station Commander's, OC Ops Wing's, OC Eng Wing's and the US Navy Commander's. The rest of us lived in Quarters in the town of Haverfordwest, some 12 miles from the airfield but only 5 miles from Little Haven.

Julie and I did not sell our house in Suffolk, but rented it out to Americans, so lived happily in a rather stark quarter in what looked just like a council estate. During the first summer in Wales our first daughter, Joanna Katherine, was born in the Haverfordwest hospital. Thus she is qualified to play rugby for Wales; she has never shown any inclination to do so. I kept a small boat in a yacht club near Milford Haven; the sailing was excellent. The summer of 1975 was a very good one, with long periods of sunshine and little rain. The two Australian girls who worked in the petrol station at Newgale, at the bottom of the hill near Brawdy, were even spotted once sunbathing topless on the roof of their garage by an eagle-eyed pilot in the circuit at Brawdy. This quickly caused the circuit to become very over-crowded!

No. 79 Squadron's operating base in the event of hostilities would have been RAF Wattisham in Suffolk, not very far from our home. Wattisham was a fighter base with a resident Lightning squadron and Phantom squadron. We much looked forward to deployments there on exercise, which occurred about twice a year. We operated our Hunters from the premises of the Anglia Gliding Club, very much in Battle of Britain style, carrying out day Combat Air Patrols about 20 to 30 miles up threat from the airfield. If we intercepted an incoming raid this usually resulted in a high-speed chase at low level, which ended up over the airfield, much to the delight of the ground crews and indeed ourselves. As soon as it got dark we packed up and went down to the Red Lion in Bildeston whilst the Lightning and

Phantom boys carried on with the war. Night flying was not one of our activities.

On one occasion, however, it became evident early on in the exercise that the OC Ops Wing wanted to exercise his *Scramble for Survival* Plan, and the only time he was going to be able to do this was after dark. The more astute of us ensured that, as twilight approached, we found our aircraft to be unserviceable. Thus it was that as dusk fell there were only two Hunters on the Operational Readiness Platform, one being flown by the Boss, George Glasgow, the other by Bo Plummer, a very experienced instructor. They were surrounded by Lightnings and Phantoms and felt somewhat overawed. *The Scramble for Survival* Plan required aircraft to get airborne, climb to an altitude determined by its position in the take-off order, establish a holding pattern over the Coltishall TACAN (Tactical Air Navigation Aid) beacon and then recover to Wattisham on reaching maximum landing fuel for an ILS approach. All this was to be done silently and without the use of radio except in emergency. It is important to understand that the Hunter had neither TACAN nor ILS.

Eventually the scramble was activated, well after sunset. Struggling to find the internal cockpit lighting our two heroes got airborne and optimistically set off towards where they thought they should go. A few minutes later there was a startled transmission from one of the Phantoms to the effect that there was an aircraft going round the holding pattern the wrong way. . . . Now it takes a long time for a Hunter with full 230 gallon tanks to burn down to landing weight and Bo Plummer's aircraft had full tanks. He went round and round the pattern until ready to recover, then let down in the general direction of Wattisham. Imagine his surprise when he broke cloud and found himself well out over the sea with no land in sight. He sensibly turned onto a westerly heading and soon picked up the lights of Great Yarmouth, and from then on it was a straightforward recovery to Wattisham. However, we were told we would not have to participate in a *Scramble for Survival* again!

Another activity of a more serious nature was the Gibraltar Detachment. The border between Spain and Gibraltar was closed in 1965 by the Spanish authorities and no aircraft inbound to Gibraltar was allowed to enter Spanish airspace, which was extremely close to Gibraltar. The Spaniards had made the arrival and departure procedures as difficult as possible and, as they claimed sovereignty over Gibraltar, theoretically it was possible that they might attempt to harass or intercept any inbound or outbound aircraft. Therefore, to defend Gibraltar's airspace and to protect both civil and military aircraft using Gibraltar, there was a permanent detachment of three Hunters and three pilots. The aircraft remained out at Gibraltar for long periods but the pilots spent only three weeks at a time, being drawn from all three squadrons at Brawdy.

We had a fairly relaxed routine, flying once or twice a day at the most, usually only when there was an inbound or outbound aircraft. At other times when aircraft were expected, we simply sat in the crewroom at some form of readiness – it was all quite relaxed as the Spanish Air Force had not tried to interfere for a long time. When airborne we used to check out the adjacent Soviet Navy anchorages for any new naval vessels, carry out a bit of air combat, support any of our own Royal Navy's warships and cooperate with any visiting detachments, often Buccaneers.

The airfield was challenging to operate from. The runway was only 6000 feet long and began and ended in the sea. There was no barrier so the brake 'chutes were essential. The Rock would produce some very difficult turbulence and cross winds in certain wind directions, which sometimes prevented flying altogether.

The social life in the evenings and at weekends was pretty hectic and it was with relief that one welcomed one's replacement off the aircraft and headed back to the UK after three weeks. During one of my 'Gib Dets' I received a phone call from the Station Commander at Brawdy informing me that I had been selected for promotion to squadron leader on the next promotion list. After recovering from the shock, I realised that this would probably mean the end of my tour on 79 Squadron. Sure enough, not long after getting back to Brawdy I learnt that I was to move on, not to a ground tour, as I had thought, but back again to Honington and No. 237 OCU, as Chief Flying Instructor.

I made the most of my last few months on 79 Squadron, which culminated in a wonderful two days at the International Air Tattoo held at Greenham Common, which celebrated twenty-five years of the Hunter. There was a superb line-up of Hunters, with the first, all red, prototype WB 188 in the centre. I had the honour to meet and chat to Sir Douglas Bader and managed to scrounge a short flight in the Battle of Britain Memorial Flight Lancaster, an unforgettable experience. Then it was back to Brawdy for the last time, to pack up the house, boat, etc, and return to the flat countryside of Suffolk, our house and back again to the Buccaneer.

CHAPTER TEN

Chief Flying Instructor, Staff College and Strike Command – 1976 to 1982

After a short refresher to re-familiarise me with my old friend the Buccaneer I took over as CFI in December 1976 from Peter Norris, who I had first met on the CFS course at Little Rissington where he was going through the same QFI course. I remember trying to sell him to a female customer one evening in the Old New Inn in Bourton on the Water, in an attempt to raise some cash to buy beer. By now he was clearly going to the top in the RAF.

The OCU was now a busy place. There were two squadrons based at Honington (12 and 208), two based at Laarbruch (15 and 16), and the last RN squadron (809) was still in commission and based at Honington when not at sea in *Ark Royal*. There was an RN Unit, loosely attached to the OCU, that looked after RN training and affairs when *Ark Royal* was at sea. Thus there was a constant stream of aircrew, both new and experienced, to put through the course. No.237 OCU had a reputation for being a hard outfit to get through, particularly for aircrew who had come from the V force. However, with no dual control version we had to insist on high standards and we were no harder on our students than the RN had been on 736 Squadron.

It seemed that many expected an easier ride than they got and so complained when they found the going tough.

My opposite number as Senior Nav Instructor was Dick Moore, a Cranwell contemporary who had gone on to Hunters after Valley but who had unfortunately lost an eye when a bird came through the canopy of his Hunter. He had retrained as a navigator and was a very good one. Our Boss was Wing Commander Arnie Parr, who was a hard taskmaster. Inevitably I spent a lot of time in the Hunter, with the associated Fam 1s in the Buccaneer, but as a Flight Commander there was now the chance to pinch one or two of the more enjoyable trips, such as the 'Bounce' for strike progression sorties. The pressure to produce trained crews was relentless and the conditions for doing so were far less suitable than they had been at Lossiemouth.

Limited availability of weapons ranges and poor weather were the two principal limiting factors that bedevilled our activities. Our safety record was remarkably good. We had one fatal accident involving our naval pilot. When away in Norway for a weekend overseas training flight, he decided to undertake some illegal low flying up a fiord on his way home, despite the protestations of his RAF navigator. He flew into high-tension cables and lost control; both ejected but only the navigator survived. The pilot drowned.

Another less traumatic but nevertheless dramatic incident occurred when a student crew set off on a routine sortie to the Wash bombing ranges. The Buccaneer's pre-take-off checks included a check by the pilot that the canopy was both closed and locked – the locking action being a separate selection to closing. The navigator observed that the aircraft was very noisy as they transited over Norfolk at 250 feet and 420 knots, but this got no reaction from the pilot, so the first clue that all was not well was missed. Once out over the sea the pilot accelerated to 550 knots to trim the aircraft out at his attack speed. He then turned towards the range. At this point the canopy, which the pilot had failed to lock in his pre-take-off checks, finally gave up and was ripped off the aircraft, embedding itself deep into the fin. The cockpit was filled with dust and a 550-knot breeze; the poor navigator could not move or speak but the pilot, protected by the front windscreen, was a bit better off. They slowed down, put out a distress call then elected to return all the way to

Honington. I was the duty instructor at the time. I was summoned to the Air Traffic Control tower and eventually the aircraft came into view, escorted by a passing Jaguar. It presented an amazing sight, as the canopy was a substantial piece of equipment, stuck half way into the fin. Apparently this highly unusual configuration did not significantly affect the aircraft's handling characteristics!

During this tour one of my Cranwell cadet contemporaries, Alastair Mathie, who had been with us at Brawdy, was based in France with an *Armée de L'Air* Jaguar squadron. He also kept his Auster at the local flying club. One day he telephoned to say that he and his wife Dot were flying back to England in the Auster. Could they land at the old airfield at Great Ashfield and stay with us for the night?

Naturally I replied yes and contacted the Bury St Edmunds police to let them know that our old airfield would be having a visitor. In due course the Auster arrived, Dot retired to the kitchen with Julie, and Alastair and I repaired to The Dog at Norton, as Alastair was desperate for a pint of proper English real ale. Meanwhile, an observant local had spotted the Auster's arrival and had walked up to the airfield to have a look, as it was rumoured that criminals had been using the airfield for refugee and drug smuggling from the continent. Ignoring the large British registration letters of G AIFG, he spotted the notice that Alastair had put on delicate parts of the airframe in French, reading '*Ne poussez pas ici*' (to dissuade Frenchmen at the flying club). The local assumed the aircraft was foreign and up to no good so he rushed home and alerted the police – sadly not the police that I had contacted but the police station at Stowmarket.

Meanwhile, in The Dog one pint had extended to three or four. Eventually back at home the ladies were disturbed by a knock on the door – it was the police, looking for Alastair and seeking an explanation! They were redirected to the Dog where eventually they were pacified. By now it was clear that driving home was not an option so the kind police offered us a lift home, which we gladly accepted. We arrived home with sirens blaring and blue lights flashing – at our insistence! The ladies were not impressed.

The summer of 1977 marked the twenty-fifth anniversary of the Queen's accession to the throne so it was decided to use twenty-five RAF aircraft in the flypast over Buckingham Palace at the end of the Trooping of the Colour Parade. The formation was to comprise two Vulcans, two Victors, two Buccaneers, two Lightnings, four Jaguars, four Phantoms and nine of the Red Arrow's Gnats. This disparate collection of aircraft, with widely differing performances and fuel states, was to be led by a Vulcan whose captain had virtually no experience of formation flying, let alone leading mixed formations over London at low level. I was to fly one of the Buccaneers in formation with the lead Vulcan. The whole unwieldy formation was to fly at 240 knots, a ridiculously low speed for the fast jets but chosen for time-keeping purposes; the V bombers were limited to remain below 300 knots at low level.

The forecast on the day was for deteriorating weather over London but the pressure was on to be there. We all formed up over Southwold and set off towards London, flying at about 1000 feet above ground level. All went well at first, but as we approached the suburbs the cloud base started to get lower and lower. Bear in mind that with the lead Vulcan at 1000 feet, and the rest all stepped down behind him, the Red Arrows right at the back were down at about 600 feet over the buildings of the East End. It was a hairy ride as it was getting turbulent. By the middle of London the cloud base was down to 1000 feet and the lead Vulcan was at 800 feet, putting the Reds down to around 400 feet.

Just after passing over the Palace all mayhem broke loose. The rearmost Victor, with two Phantoms on each side, got too close to the Victor ahead and pushed down to avoid collision, thereby putting itself right in the face of the nine Gnats. At the same moment the leading Vulcan went into thick cloud. The Reds broke away, descended as low as they dared and raced off over west London back to their home base at Kemble. The Jaguars, Lightnings and Phantoms, by now in cloud, all broke away from their V bombers, engaged afterburners and split up, climbing for safety in the middle of the busy London Control Zone. My No. 2 and I managed to stick on the wing of our Vulcan as it stumbled up through the thick turbulent cloud; the cloud was so dense that I could only see a small portion of the Vulcan's enormous wing. It was the most frightening situation I had been in for a long time, especially as we were flying so slowly. We had no idea what had happened to the rest of the formation. Eventually we broke out of cloud somewhere well to the north of London, only to see the Vulcan that had originally been behind us out ahead by a mile or so. Somehow it had overtaken us in cloud – how close it had come we will never know. We recovered back to Honington thankful that we had survived and I swore never to get involved in flypasts over London again, a commitment I was subsequently unable to honour. The photo taken from the ground as we flew over the Palace does not show the chaos that was about to occur.

During this tour the RN finally finished their Buccaneer flying in 1978 and our small RN Unit was disbanded. The 809 Squadron aircraft were handed back to the RAF, repainted in RAF colours and eventually another RAF squadron was expected to form at Honington. This was to be 216 Squadron, a unit that had previously only ever flown transport aircraft. Coincidental with this unit's re-formation was the introduction of another new weapon system into the inventory, the Pavespike laser designation pod and the laser-guided bomb. The introduction of this equipment did not affect our activities on 237 OCU at this time but it would do in the future.

In 1977 the first RAF participation in the USAF's Red Flag exercise took place, again a first for the Buccaneer. We sent our Qualified Weapons Instructor course along on the first Red Flag, along with an instructor crew. The Americans were astonished at the way in which the British operated their aircraft and were somewhat mortified to find out that our tactics of flying at high speed and ultra low level were extremely successful when compared with their more restrained approach.

In 1979, as my time on 237 OCU was coming to an end, the first fatal accident involving structural failure of a Buccaneer wing occurred. In this incident the latch pin, which held the folding section of the wing in place, failed on a German-based aircraft with fatal consequences. All latch pins were replaced and the fleet was soon flying again, but not for long. In January 1980 there was another fatal accident during a Red Flag exercise; in this case the wing failed in the inner non-folding section owing to metal fatigue. The whole fleet was grounded with little prospect of an early return to flying status. Thus it was not too hard a pill to swallow when I left Honington for the now inevitable desk jobs; at least it was to be via a year at the RAF Staff College, Bracknell.

*   *   *

This promised to be an interesting and demanding year, both intellectually and socially, so we packed up the house again and went off to school in Berkshire. Staff College was indeed an interesting year away from flying. At the end of the course it was time for postings; by this time my old Station Commander, the Bear, had been promoted to Air Marshal and was looking for a Personal Staff Officer (PSO). Thus it was that I was posted to Headquarters Strike Command, RAF High Wycombe, as PSO to the Deputy Commander in Chief. The next eighteen months were a frantic whirlwind of activity. There was no ADC to take up the load of running the Air Marshal's residence and social programme, so this work had to be dovetailed with all the outer office work. There was also no flying, apart from as a passenger with the Air Marshal.

The Falklands War took place in the middle of this tour; it was strange to be a bystander whilst the action unfolded, but being present whilst the most senior of the RAF's Commanders debated what to do. It became increasingly obvious from the intelligence reports that the Argentines were going to invade the Falklands, but the inaction from the government, who must have been given the same intelligence, was difficult to understand. In the end we won, but it was a close run thing; I heard the news in a VC 10 over Greenland as we returned from a visit to the USAF in Omaha, Nebraska.

Overall it was a tough tour, which I did not enjoy, but thankfully there was the occasional amusing incident, but they were few and far between. Two I recall both involved the Commander in Chief, Air Chief Marshal Sir Keith Williamson, whose residence was some distance away from the Headquarters. One evening, whilst watching the evening TV news, my phone rang; it was the Bear, claiming that he had heard intruders prowling in his garden. He demanded that I summon the RAF Police to investigate; why he could not have done this himself I still do not know. I duly telephoned the police guard post and told them to go to the DC-in-C's residence immediately to investigate intruders. Unfortunately the sleepy police corporal thought I said 'the C-in-C's residence' and sent his gallant team off into the Buckinghamshire countryside, where eventually they awoke a very surprised Air Chief Marshal who sent them away with a flea in their ears. Meanwhile I received a series of increasingly enraged phone calls from the Bear demanding to know where the police had got to. Eventually whoever it was disappeared from his garden and peace returned – until the next morning!

The second incident occurred one morning in February. We were supposed to go to Honington for the official opening of the Tornado Weapons Conversion Unit, the Bear having decided to present a large silver bowl as a prize for the best student on the course. Unfortunately, over night there was a really heavy snow fall of about two feet depth; as a consequence all the roads around High Wycombe were virtually impassable. Thus our plan to drive to RAF Northolt in order to fly to Honington seemed doomed to failure. However, the C-in-C had the use of the only four-wheel drive vehicle in the High Wycombe MT Section, a rather ancient Land Rover that was provided to get him from his residence to the Headquarters in inclement weather. After the C-in-C's arrival that morning – in the aforesaid Land Rover – the Bear stole the keys. Without telling the C-in-C or any of his staff we set off for Northolt, me sitting in the back under the canvas tilt, clutching the silver bowl and two RAF swords, clad in a greatcoat, with the Bear and his Cpl driver in the front.

The journey to Northolt normally took about thirty-five minutes; today, because of the snow and appalling traffic congestion, it took two and a half very cold hours. This was before the days of mobile phones so we were out of contact with the Headquarters for the whole journey. The C-in-C, wanting to go home for lunch, discovered his transport had been hijacked and not surprisingly flew into a rage. When we arrived at Northolt, we were met by a very agitated Station Commander, who announced that the C-in-C wished to speak to the Bear *very urgently*.

The Bear disappeared into the terminal building, only to emerge a few moments later looking grim. We returned to High Wycombe in a frosty silence. As we drove up the hill towards the Headquarters, the Bear suddenly announced that he was feeling indisposed and that he would be going directly back to his residence. I was charged with returning the Land Rover to its rightful owner, the C-in-C! Luckily, after an initial explosion, the C-in-C realised that I was merely an innocent bystander in the plot so did not blame me, but I believe he and the Bear had an icy exchange of views when they met the next morning!

* * *

One of the consequences of the Falklands War was a considerable turbulence in personnel, with the need for people to be sent down south to run the new establishment in the Falkland Islands. In September 1982 I discovered I was to move again, this time with the acting rank of wing commander, to a completely new world at the Headquarters of Support Command, at Brampton in Cambridgeshire. It was another ground tour, but with the distinct chance of flying two new aircraft. I was to be the staff officer responsible for all aspects of fast jet advanced flying training on the Hawk at Valley and multi-engine advanced flying training at Finningley. So I said my farewells to the Bear and Strike Command, went down to Brawdy for a week's familiarisation with the Hawk and then moved into quarters at RAF Brampton.

CHAPTER ELEVEN

Hawk, Jetstream and (Again) Buccaneer – 1982 to 1987

The Hawk was a great little aircraft, agile and responsive, but positively a trainer rather than a front-line aircraft like the Hunter. I found out that I was responsible for all the activities at RAF Valley, where all Support Command's Hawk flying, apart from the Red Arrows, took place. This meant I had to make regular visits to Anglesey and naturally that involved flying whenever possible. It was great to get back in the cockpit again. Valley had not changed much since my earlier time there with the Gnat, however, with the excellent serviceability of the Hawk it was a very busy place. The Hawk had a far greater endurance than the Gnat so more ambitious sorties were possible. The view from the back seat was excellent; you were hardly aware of the pilot in front of you, a far cry from the cramped and limited view from the back of a Gnat. I soon settled into the routine of the staff work associated with Valley, which was much more pleasant than running around looking after an Air Marshal.

The other part of the work covered multi-engine flying training on the Jetstream, a twin turbo-prop trainer aircraft originally designed as a light commuter airliner. The Jetstream had an inauspicious start to its career as a trainer in the RAF, culminating in its withdrawal from service and being placed in storage, but by 1982 it was back in service again and working properly. It was a completely different sort of flying to what I had been used to and it was my first experience of using a turbo prop. I went 'solo', but with another pilot in the right-hand seat, and so collected another type in my logbook. The Jetstream aspect of my tour provided some interesting variety and entertainment. Weekend support for the Red Arrows was one activity that I enjoyed, as there were few volunteers to fly around the UK in pursuit of the team, carrying spares and a few ground crew.

At this time there was a proposal to bring Ground Launched Cruise Missiles into the UK, based at Greenham Common in Berkshire. This generated a furious response from the Campaign for Nuclear Disarmament and the peace camp full of horrible women that grew up outside the gates became notorious in the national press. I found myself assisting a Group Captain in devising a plan for the security of the site, so in order to circumnavigate the monstrous regiment of women at the front gate we used our own Jetstream to fly in and out.

One consequence of this work was that we were privy to the highly classified information as to when the first missiles were due to be flown in to the site from the USA. This was information that the peace campers would have loved to have had, as they were threatening to invade the site when it happened. Imagine our consternation when the date was revealed in a national Sunday newspaper; had we been lax with our security? As it turned out we were blameless, as the information had been leaked to the paper by a London-based female civil servant, but we did sweat for a bit.

Late in the autumn of 1983, after only a year at Brampton, I got a phone call from the Bear advising me that I had been selected to command 237 OCU, but not to tell anyone yet as it was still to be confirmed. When the news came out officially I was delighted. My boss was furious but there was nothing he could do. I then caught mumps – not nice at the age of forty-one! Thus my second ground tour came to an end after only eighteen, months in which I had become qualified on two new aircraft and had clocked up quite a number of flying hours.

* * *

By early 1984 the Buccaneer Force had changed considerably from what it had been when I left it in early 1980. After the wing failure accident in the USA the number of serviceable aircraft had reduced significantly and there were only enough for two front-line squadrons and an OCU. The two squadrons based in Germany had been disbanded and re-formed as Tornado squadrons. The two remaining squadrons, 12 and 208, were now both based at Lossiemouth and were committed specifically to the maritime attack role. The OCU was still located at Honington but was due to move in late 1984 to join the squadrons at Lossiemouth.

I started my refresher flying in May 1984 and almost immediately became involved with a Board of Inquiry into a fatal accident that occurred at Lossiemouth on 208 Squadron. This was a particularly unhappy affair, which made a deep impression on me, particularly in respect of the need for squadron members to have trust in their commanding officer, such that they felt able to discuss their personal problems with him when need be. Overall, it was a very messy business but we managed to avoid the next of kin suffering unnecessary hurt.

Once that was over I completed my refresher and took over the unit from the indefatigable Wing Commander David Mulinder in September. No sooner had I taken command, when arrangements for us to move north really began to gather pace. There was going to be a considerable amount of domestic upheaval for all concerned; we were going to have to leave our house and move to a married quarter that was pretty much identical to the local council houses! Our squadron accommodation was also going through a major renovation but was the same building that had been used by 736 Squadron when Lossiemouth was a naval airfield – it was good to be back in the old building doing the same thing again!

One thing I will never forget was our Dining Out from Honington. The boys constructed a large Buccaneer out of cardboard, about 8 feet long, equipped with a rocket-launching tube under each wing. A long electrical cable connected the launching tubes to a 12-volt car battery. An initial trial firing in the empty squadron building was truly spectacular, with the rockets exploding violently on impact with the wall. The initial reaction was that it was too dangerous to use it in the Officers' Mess, but, after a few beers before the event, the boys changed their mind. It was duly suspended from the ceiling of the dining room, with the car battery hidden beneath the table. Despite the attempts of the Mess Staff to have it removed, it survived and we all sat down to dine with it hanging menacingly over us.

On my left was the Boss of the Tornado Weapons Conversion Unit. He asked what the Buccaneer was going to do – I explained that it would be pulled along the rail from which it was suspended and that it would dump a large amount of talcum powder on whoever was below – which happened to be him. He was not amused and we didn't converse very much for the rest of the evening. On my right was OC Ops Wing. He too asked what the Buccaneer would do – I told him to get down under the table as soon as I had completed my speech – good advice, as it turned out.

When my turn came to speak, I made an appropriately rabble-rousing speech vilifying the Tornado and extolling the virtues of the Buccaneer. When I finished speaking the switch was thrown on the battery. There was a suitably theatrical pause, which convinced the diners that it wasn't going to work, then the rockets went off. They spread all over the dining room, exploding loudly wherever they hit. How no one was injured I will never know. About three or four hit the door leading to the kitchens, which was severely damaged as a consequence. Behind the door was a lady carrying a large tray of glasses from the dishwasher to the cupboards; when the rockets struck she dropped the entire tray load and screamed loudly, thereby enhancing the whole effect of the event. The whole dining room erupted with a standing ovation, which was a most gratifying and fitting way to end the Buccaneer's association with RAF Honington.

The rest of the evening has disappeared from my memory in an alcoholic haze, but inscribed in my logbook is the following statement, written by the Station Commander, Group Captain Peter Harding:

As 237 OCU is relocated at RAF Lossiemouth, the Buccaneer era comes to an end at Honington after 15 years. My best wishes to you and 237 for a successful time at Lossiemouth , thank you for all your help both in the air and on the ground during a trouble-free move North. We shall remember the Guest Night for ever, the scars will not remain for quite so long.

Running 237 OCU at Lossiemouth was a great pleasure. The weather was very good, we had weapons ranges right on our doorstep, the vast low-flying area in the north of Scotland was always available and I had an excellent team of instructors and ground crew. We were only training crews for 12 and 208 Squadrons, who were both resident with us at Lossiemouth. The airfield was a busy place as in addition to the three Buccaneer squadrons there was the Jaguar OCU, a detachment of 22 Squadron flying search and rescue Sea Kings and last but by no means least 8 Squadron with its mighty Shackletons. Friday nights in the Officers' Mess Bar were noisy and exciting.

Although all the Buccaneer squadrons belonged to 18 Group, the maritime element of Strike Command, 237 OCU was given an interesting and unique war role, which had nothing to do with maritime operations. When the Buccaneer squadrons were withdrawn from RAF Germany in 1984 there was no unit in that theatre of operations that could undertake airborne laser designation for aircraft carrying laser-guided bombs. A number of important operational plans required the use of airborne laser designation, so as 237 OCU had a number of navigators who were very experienced in overland Buccaneer operations, it was given the task of supporting the Jaguar and Tornado squadrons in Germany in war time. This required regular visits to Laarbruch to work with the resident squadrons. Not surprisingly, HQ 18 Group were not particularly enthusiastic about this activity as it would have liked to have had all Buccaneers assigned to maritime operations. However, we were determined to carry on with this work, ably supported in HQ 2 ATAF by Group Captain Nigel Walpole, who had once been an OC 12 Squadron, and was a great enthusiast for our overland capabilities. It also gave the squadron a unique ethos, which was much preferable to simply supporting the other two squadrons at Lossiemouth.

The technique we used for low-level overland laser designation was as follows. Two Buccaneers, loaded with a Pavespike designator pod, a Sidewinder AAM, an underwing tank, an electronic countermeasures (ECM) jamming pod and four 1000-lb bombs with retard tails (in the bomb door), would get airborne either with the laser bomb-armed aircraft, or would *rendezvous* once airborne. Each Buccaneer would formate with a section of bombers. The Tornado crews initially doubted whether the Buccaneers could keep up with them, especially in the event of an abort from low level due to bad weather; but we soon disproved this notion!

During the final approach run to the target it was essential for the Buccaneer pilot to identify the target and place his HUD aiming mark on it so that the navigator, who before take-off had aligned his laser designator aiming symbol (displayed on his TV screen) with the pilot's HUD aiming mark, could also identify the target on his head down screen. Once the navigator had done this he called 'happy', thereby allowing his pilot to manoeuvre, at up to 4 g, away from the target. This was usually achieved at a range of between 5 to 2 miles from the target, depending on the size of the target and the visibility.

The Pavespike pod could only be carried on the Buccaneer's port inner wing pylon, so all turns away from the target had to be to the right, to allow the pod's head to stay in line of sight with the target for the maximum amount of time. It was essential for the navigator to continue to track the target manually with his pod. This was no easy feat at 4 g, with his head down peering into a TV screen, controlling his marker with a primitive thumb-operated control.

Weapon release from the bombers was indicated either by a call of 'bombs gone' or a tone transmission on the radio. The subsequent timing of firing the laser was absolutely critical; firing too soon would result in a big undershoot as the bomb tried to guide direct to the target, but firing too late would result in an overshoot. Nevertheless, despite these difficulties and the lack of range facilities to conduct live firing practice (only Garve Island Range, near Cape Wrath, could be used and it was only available for very limited periods) the results achieved were very impressive.

The Buccaneer was the only RAF aircraft capable of providing stand-off airborne laser designation from 1979 (when Pavespike was first introduced) until 1991, when the TIALD pod finally came into service on the Tornado. Should the formation be engaged *en route* the Buccaneers were well able to defend themselves, with their Sidewinder AAM, chaff packets (loaded into the airbrake), the ECM pod and the four retard 1000-lb bombs, which could be used as a 'last ditch' defence against a fighter carrying out an attack from astern. It is interesting to note that the Buccaneer's major operational contribution to the Gulf War of 1991 was as airborne laser designators, albeit from high level rather than the low-level scenario for which we practised so much.

A by-product of this activity was the opportunity to become involved in the NATO squadron exchange scheme. A Dutch F16 squadron (322), based at Leeuwarden, was equipped to carry Laser Guided Bombs (LGBs) and with the assistance of Nigel Walpole we organised a squadron exchange with them. The Dutch were very keen to toss some of their LGBs at Garve Island, the Cape Wrath weapons range, as there was nowhere in Holland where they could do this. We were naturally going to provide the laser designation for them, thereby giving a graphic demonstration of true NATO interoperability.

Two Buccaneers and two F16s set off for Garve. The weather was good and I had an expert Pavespike operator, Norman Browne, as my navigator. The live toss bombing exercise was a great success with all the F16s' bombs guiding well and impacting on target. Norman even managed to organise an HF radio link to Nigel Walpole in his office in Germany to tell him of our success. So far, so good.

The plan was then to fly across the 'moon country' in the north of Scotland, escorted by the two F16s, to be bounced by a third F16. The 'bounce' duly turned up. Our two Buccaneers accelerated off leaving the three Dutchmen to indulge in a bit of air combat. Half an hour later we were sat in the debrief, watching the Pavespike videos, when a broadcast from Air Traffic Control announced that an F16 was returning to the circuit with engine handling problems . . . it was our bounce aircraft, which had got airborne somewhat later than us. A few moments later Air Traffic announced that the aircraft had landed safely and we went back to our debrief.

Suddenly, the door to the briefing room burst open revealing an incandescant F16 pilot, gibbering away in what can only be described as Double Dutch. All the remaining Dutchmen immediately leapt to their feet and rushed out upstairs to their detachment office, slamming the door shut behind them. Sounds of considerable altercation came from behind the closed door. At this point my Warrant Officer, Jack Sim, sidled up to me. 'I think you had better come out to the flight line and have a look at this F16' he said. The F16 had a thin wisp of vapour coming out of its jet pipe. Closer inspection revealed that the entire back end of the aircraft was riddled with 20-mm bullet holes. 'Get it into the hangar as quick as you can' I said to Jack.

By now the Dutch had calmed down somewhat and were able to offer an explanation. After leaving the bombing range one of the pilots had failed to put his master armament switch to safe. Dutch F16s always flew with a full load of 20-mm ball ammunition, apparently to keep the Centre of Gravity within limits. Our pilot found himself in a position to claim a shot at the F16 ahead of him. He selected air to air, pressed the trigger to film his opponent, and because his master arm switch was still live the gun fired. Luckily he was only tracking the rear of the aircraft ahead, not the cockpit as is normal. However, seeing that nothing appeared amiss with his opponent, he decided to say nothing and carried on with the fight! His opponent, unaware of what had happened, carried on with his sortie and only became aware that something was not quite right when he rejoined the circuit. The Dutch decided to lock up their miscreant pilot in the detachment office for the rest of the day/night.

I went to see the Station Commander, Group Captain Bruce Latton, to brief him on the affair. His immediate and understandable reaction was that we should tell someone; I urged caution. After all, the incident took place over moon country and was unlikely to have been witnessed by anyone. The Dutch were doubtless going to take care of their culprit in their own way. If anyone brought in a dead sheep riddled with 20-mm ammunition, or even a dead human, we could always claim that the incident was under investigation. Eventually the Station Commander agreed; we left it to the Dutch to sort out. The culprit was flown back to Holland the next day in handcuffs and the F16 underwent an engine change in our hangar.

No one from moon country complained and the incident was quietly forgotten. However, I could not resist mentioning at the final Dining In Night for the Dutchmen, that when the RAF shot themselves down they did it properly. (Earlier in the year a Phantom shot down a Jaguar recovering into Bruggen.) Our next squadron exchange was with a Portuguese Air Force squadron and was an altogether much more restrained affair.

A once in a lifetime opportunity occurred in 1986 when I was given permission to display the Hunter T7 at a number of air displays and unit events during the summer. I embarked on a work up programme that saw my minimum height for aerobatics steadily come down from the usual 5000 feet above ground to a minimum of 500 feet for aerobatics and 200 feet for level passes. The work up was greatly assisted by having a trusty navigator beside me – in most cases Bob Poots – who was a great help providing lookout to the right, timing and reminders of next manoeuvre, height and speeds. Finally the day came for the check out by the AOC; the first attempt failed due to the cockpit being full of water after an overnight rain storm, which drenched everything during the pre display inverted flight check. The second go was successful.

Bob and I subsequently displayed at a number of events, including the Lossiemouth Air Day, the St Mawgan, St Athan and Abingdon Air Shows and a number of lesser events. It was great fun and the beautifully mannered Hunter never let us down. No. 237 OCU even put up a five-aircraft Hunter formation team for the Lossiemouth Air Day. After a few passes in different formations I broke off for my solo. It was probably the last time a military Hunter team displayed in the UK.

We were encouraged to get to know the other squadrons and their work so I decided to learn about flying the Shackleton with 8 Squadron. This was something quite different. I needed two cushions behind me and two underneath me to reach the controls and see out. The aircraft was a great heavy brute to fly; it had to be landed on three points or it would bounce down the runway with increasing severity. Piston engine handling was a complete mystery to me at that time. Nevertheless I was launched off 'solo' by day and collected a first pilot day qualification in my logbook.

Eventually the good life of flying, skiing, sailing and exploring Scotland was bound to come to an end. Much to my amazement and delight a posting came through to CFS at RAF Scampton as Officer Commanding Examining Wing, another flying tour as the chief trapper! Two flying tours as a wing commander was almost too good to be true but I had the posting notice in my hand and could hardly believe my luck. I was sad to leave Lossiemouth as I would almost certainly not fly the Buccaneer again. After over 2000 hours on type, plus over 1000 hours on the Hunter in associated flying, it was a wrench to get out of such a fine aircraft probably for the last time. I retained a war role appointment back on 237 OCU but the chances of using it to fly the Buccaneer again were very remote. So yet again we packed our bags and set off down to Lincolnshire, the first time I had been based there since leaving Cranwell in 1963, twenty-four years previously.

CHAPTER TWELVE

CFS Examining Wing, Brampton and Linton-on-Ouse – 1987 to 1994

My responsibilities as OC Examining Wing covered a very wide parish,ranging from quality control of the flying clubs that provided flying scholarships for seventeen-year-old schoolchildren, to standards of instruction at OCUs and on front-line squadrons. There was so much to get involved with that choices had to be made. As I had a fast jet background I started with a Hawk conversion course to gain an instructional qualification, then I moved to the Jetstream for a similar qualification. Then a familiarisation with the piston-engined Bulldog followed. Then one with the Jet Provost, some twenty-four years after my initial flying training. The rotary wing instructional business was also one of my responsibilities; this allowed me to go on a senior officer's acquaint course on the Gazelle helicopter, lasting only a week. However, despite the short time available I managed to go solo, something I enjoyed more than anything I had previously experienced in aviation. At the other end of the scale were the gliders used by the Air Training Corps, one powered by a small engine, the others pure sailplanes –

another delightful aviation experience that I was privileged to experience.

There were also many trips abroad at the invitation of foreign air forces. After an often long flight and arriving in unfamiliar territory, one was presented with the Pilot's Notes of an aircraft previously never flown, and expected next morning to perform as an examiner, with all the authority of the Royal Air Force Central Flying School. In my two years at CFS I flew in the Oman, Jordan, Kenya, Switzerland, Singapore and Dubai; I flew a variety of unusual aircraft including the F5, Macchi 326 and 329, SF 260 Warrior, Defender, Skyvan, S211, Hawk 61 and a microlight called the Skywalker.

Flying in the Oman with the Sultan of Oman's Air Force (SOAF), now called the Royal Air Force of Oman, was particularly memorable. In the short space of ten days I flew the Defender and Skyvan for the first time and renewed my acquaintance with both the single- and two-seat Hunter.

One afternoon a group of RAF and SOAF aircrew climbed aboard two Skyvans, flew over the Jebel Akhdar to the empty desert, selected a suitably smooth-looking bit of terrain and landed. We then proceeded to fill a large number of empty beer tins with petrol from jerrycans, place a wick in the tins' openings, then lay them out on the desert floor to outline a runway. Whilst the sun went down we sat under the wings of the Skyvans, eating a delicious curry that had been brought out in 'hot locks'. Once it was dark we lit the wicks in the beer cans, started up the aircraft, got airborne and flew a few circuits on our beer can- illuminated desert strip until the flames finally went out. Then we returned to base in time for a last beer before the Mess bar closed. Wonderful!

It was also quite sobering to land on a primitive strip right up on the border with Yemen. We would taxi back slowly to the take-off point whilst dropping off passengers and freight 'on the move', then get airborne again whilst watching the Yemeni ZSU23/4 anti-aircraft gun batteries just over the border, and very close to the strip, tracking our every move.

Flying in Jordan was another unusual experience. The airfield that was the F5 base was called H5, situated not too far from the Iraqi border. The two-seat F5 had a very poor view from the back seat so we were asked not to attempt any landings, to save us the embarrassment of a rear-end strike on the runway.

Needless to say one of the pilots that I flew with allowed the rear end to contact the runway and the damage, in the shape of two seriously scraped jet pipes that were no longer circular, was obvious. That individual didn't fly with us again but next morning the aircraft was back on the flight line, the damage having been beaten out with a hide-face hammer.

We were provided with a very ancient refrigerator in our sparse accommodation for our beer supply, but it did not have an electric plug attached. Our host simply stuffed the two wires into a wall socket to make it work. After a shower and whilst still damp I tried to open the door to extract a beer, only to be blown across the room by a large electric shock as the whole refrigerator was live. We removed the wire from the socket by tying a bootlace to it and pulling it out. Our post flying beers remained at room temperature from then onwards.

Back in the UK I expanded my fast jet experience to include the Phantom FGR2. I achieved this with just two flights at the Phantom OCU at Leuchars, courtesy of the Boss, Dave Roume. I found the Phantom to be technically very similar to the Buccaneer. It had a much greater performance but was much twitchier at high speed and at low level.

I quite unexpectedly gained a first pilot (night) qualification in the mighty Shackleton. This came about as a result of a phone call from Wg Cdr Dave Hencken, who commanded the Shackleton squadron. He explained that he had been posted to Brussels but if he arrived with a current QFI category he would be able to instruct at the local flying club. Could I help? I said yes, a trip in a Jet Provost would be sufficient. However, he asked that if he could send me solo at night in the Shackleton would that do? I said yes, wonderful, but when? He replied that he would be shortly on his way to Coningsby and to meet him there at 8 pm. There was now no way I could get out of this so I set off across Lincolnshire in my car and sure enough, when I got to Coningsby in the dusk there was the Shackleton waiting for me.

After four or five rather shaky night circuits and landings in the great beast I said to Dave that I was quite happy to sign his logbook there and then. He, however, insisted on sending me off on my own, with a rather reluctant co-pilot in the right-hand seat and a bunch of probably terrified rear crew down the back, for the required four circuits and landings. It was now completely dark and the sensation was exactly the same as it would have been flying a Lancaster in World War Two – blue flames from the Griffons' exhausts, the pneumatic brakes hissing and squealing, ancient flight instruments dimly lit in red light. It was an unforgettable experience. Luckily I completed the sortie without damaging anything, achieving four good three-point landings and taxiing back successfully (quite a challenge with pneumatic brakes). I signed Dave's logbook, he signed mine and we went our separate ways. As I drove back to Scampton in the dark I realised it was the anniversary of the Dambusters' raid. Local legend had it that the ghost of Guy Gibson's dog Nigger was seen running round Scampton on this occasion – so I hurried back home as quickly as possible but saw nothing!

Another interesting aspect of the job was the requirement to fly with the Red Arrows once a year during their pre-season work up to check that they could handle emergencies correctly and safely whilst in formation displays. This was exciting if somewhat nerve-racking work, especially as the Team were going through a period when they suffered a number of accidents.

The RAF's new basic trainer, the Tucano, also made its appearance for the first time at Scampton in 1988. Powered by a turbo prop and with seats one behind the other, it represented a complete change from the Jet Provost that it was replacing. The cockpit was supposed to be virtually the same as the Hawk's, thereby easing transition from one aircraft to another. The Tucano was quite a sprightly performer up to 240 knots but it ran out of steam at that point. The engine control system was complex and not very reliable and the build quality left much to be desired initially. It was an interesting challenge bringing into service such a different type of trainer; many people regretted the passing of the simple and reliable Jet Provost. In spite of being hyped as having jet-like handling qualities, the Tucano was not jet-like at all. Nevertheless it was nice to have another aircraft in my logbook, especially a brand-new one.

The two and a half years at Scampton simply raced by and toward the end of 1989 it looked like another move was on the cards. This time it had to be a ground tour and so it was, albeit with a promotion to Group Captain. As a final fling, in early December 1989 we took a Jetstream full of CFS staff to Berlin for a long weekend, sending our wives on ahead by civil airliner. The Berlin Wall had just come down and the collapse of the East German regime was under way; it was going to be an interesting visit. We had to refuel on the way at RAF Wildenrath in order to arrive at Berlin with sufficient fuel for a return to Hanover. I taxied the Jetstream out to the holding point, parked and applied the handbrake, which was exactly the same style as those fitted to early 1950s Ford Popular cars.

After receiving our airways clearance I attempted to release the parking brake, but to no avail. It was stuck firmly on. Sqn Ldr Fred Da Costa, my large and very strong co-pilot and Jetstream expert, was also unable to release it. Visions of our unsupervised wives spending huge sums of money in Berlin, whilst we languished unserviceable at Wildenrath for the weekend, floated before our eyes. A member of the Wildenrath Visiting Aircraft Flight was summoned to the aircraft. He could not, or would not, offer any advice or assistance. At this point Fred removed from his flying suit an enormous Swiss Army penknife. He ordered the ground crew to undo the screws that held on the panel into which the handbrake lever disappeared. This was done, somewhat reluctantly, and our visiting assistant disappeared. Fred then pulled out the split pin that connected the handbrake lever to the operating cables of the handbrake, thereby releasing the handbrake, allowing us to proceed. It was a strange sensation, accelerating down the runway with the handbrake lever still firmly on!

We had a most interesting weekend in Berlin, watching the Berlin Wall being destroyed and realising that we were witnessing the probable end of the Cold War era. We returned the Jetstream to Finningley, explaining briefly the handbrake saga and leaving before we were asked any more questions.

I returned to RAF Brampton as Group Captain Flying Training, an appointment that held responsibility for all the flying training activity within what was then called RAF Support Command. Given my recent wide experience of flying within the Command it was a logical and sensible move. I had a large office in the corner of the Headquarters building with a good view of the helipad. I had a large staff of officers ranging from flight lieutenant up to wing commander working for me and, by and large, the work was interesting.

There were forays out of the office to the flying training stations, which always involved flying, especially as I had been current at Scampton in all the Command's training aircraft. Shortly after my arrival the man from the Jetstream office came in to talk about some unauthorised tampering with a Jetstream handbrake that had occurred on an overseas training flight – luckily I was able to tell him I knew all about it and had the matter in hand!

Just down the road at Cambridge Airport, Cambridge University Air Squadron were short of a QFI. Cambridge Airport was on the way home so I was kindly taken on as a part-time instructor, flying there whenever I could get a morning or afternoon away from the office.

After my experience over London in 1977 I had hoped never to become involved with this sort of flypast ever again, but not long after arriving at Brampton I was detailed off to organise the airborne element of the Queen Mother's ninetieth birthday celebrations that were to take place on Horse Guards Parade in the centre of London. The event was a celebration, not a military parade with fixed timings. The organiser, a gentleman called Major Parker, was insistent that the flypast should take place at the correct time but he was unable to tell me what that time would be. However, there would be a two-minute 'window' in which all flypast participants would be required to pass in front of the Queen Mother.

The elements of the flypast were the outfits that had the Queen Mother as patron, namely the Army Air Corps Historic Flight, the Royal Navy Historic Flight, the Battle of Britain Memorial Flight and the Central Flying School. Thus there was a wide range of aircraft performance to cope with, ranging from the 90 knots of the Army Air Corps Historic Flight, through the 180 knots of the Battle of Britain Memorial Flight to the 360 knots of the nine Central Flying School Hawks. This presented me with a big planning challenge, especially as there was only the two-minute window available. Clearly it was essential to have an idea as to how the celebration was progressing in order to know when to send the various aircraft with their wide range of speeds out of their holding patterns to achieve their overhead time. The Army kindly offered the use of a Clansman radio set, reputedly man portable, for a man on the ground to communicate directly with the formations.

I decided we would have to try this piece of kit out 'in situ', so the Army provided a Lynx helicopter, which flew me and one of my squadron leaders into the Honourable Artillery Company's landing site in the City. We then took a taxi to Horse Guards, lugging the extremely heavy Clansman radio with us. On arriving at Horse Guards, which was thronged with tourists, we set up the radio. We attempted to talk to our Lynx, which was now hovering just overhead. We were completely unsuccessful in achieving two-way communication, much to the tourists' amusement, so we retired back to the helicopter landing site to think again.

Then my squadron leader had a brilliant idea. Mobile phones were becoming quite common by this time, so he suggested that he should position himself on the parade ground, equipped with a mobile phone and in constant communication with RAF Northolt Air Traffic Control. All the flypast aircraft would also be on Northolt's radar frequency, so we could get an almost instant update on what was going on at Horse Guards. This plan worked out very well.

I hitched a ride in the leading Hawk because I wanted to be there in case there were problems on the day. In the event all went well, and all the aircraft made it into the two-minute window. Unfortunately we were all slightly early and overflew the celebration whilst the bands were playing 'Land of Hope and Glory'; not what the gallant Major had planned but very appropriate nonetheless. Evidently the crowd loved it.

The Hawk formation landed at RAF Abingdon and arrived at the bar just in time to watch the event on the 10 o'clock news.

Some nine months after starting at Brampton the situation in the Middle East deteriorated rapidly with the Iraqi invasion of Kuwait and it was soon clear that a medium-scale war was going to be inevitable. In December 1990 I was told to put together a plan that involved moving medical teams around the UK in our Jetstream and Domine training aircraft to meet incoming aircraft with battle casualties on board who needed to be categorised and sent on to appropriate hospitals and treatment centres. We were told to expect a jumbo jet-sized aircraft in every hour within twenty-four hours of the outbreak of hostilities – anywhere within the UK. This was going to be quite a challenge to meet and would have involved the cessation of all multi-engine pilot training and all navigator training.

In the end the plan was never activated because of the very long air campaign, followed by a very short land campaign, which produced minimal casualties. However, I did get involved in some support flying activity associated with the Gulf War. Once hostilities commenced there was a need to fly staff from the Joint Air Reconnaissance and Intelligence Centre (JARIC), also located at Brampton, out to Ramstein Air Base in Germany to collect intelligence material and then return them speedily to JARIC. We used a Jetstream for this task, flying out of and returning to Wyton, which was just up the road from Brampton.

This was yet another chance to grab a bit of flying as many of these tasks were flown in the evenings. The two spooks would sit in the back of the Jetstream, then disappear on arrival at Ramstein. Sometimes we would only be on the ground for fifteen minutes, sometimes for more than two hours, before they returned clutching bags, which they held onto tightly.

On one occasion the whole of the south-east of England became covered in fog when we returned. We failed to get into Wyton (it was now approaching midnight), but Marham was still open and we managed to scrape in there. The Station Commander, Group Captain Jock Stirrup (later to become Chief of the Air Staff) kindly offered us a car to run us all back to Brampton, which the co-pilot and I gladly accepted. The spooks refused the offer and waited for their own special transport to come and collect them. Clearly whatever they had collected from Ramstein was very valuable!

The war was won in fairly quick time and life at the Headquarters slipped back into its usual routine, although an impending planned move of all staffs down to Innsworth began to attract our attention.

Luckily fate intervened again in the form of yet another posting back to flying, this time as Station Commander of RAF Linton-on-Ouse and Officer Commanding No. 1 Flying Training School. So after a mere twenty-two months at Brampton I was on the move again, this time to Yorkshire after a quick Jet Provost refresher course at CFS. Linton-on-Ouse had always had a wonderful reputation as a first class Station and it certainly lived up to its name. It was built during the RAF's expansion in the 1930s, so was a well-founded establishment with substantial buildings. The Station Commander's residence, Whitley House, was a large detached house with a huge garden that we were swallowed up in.

In addition to the airfield at Linton, I was also responsible for the operation of no fewer than three other airfields used as relief landing grounds – Church Fenton, Topcliffe and Dishforth. The Royal Navy Elementary Flying Training Squadron (RNEFTS) was based at Topcliffe so my connections with the Fleet Air Arm were happily re-established. No. 1 Flying Training School was equipped with two types of Jet Provost, the elderly Mk 3a and the slightly younger Mk 5a. RNEFTS flew the Bulldog and it was not long before the first Tucano arrived from Church Fenton to replace the Jet Provosts. Finally there was a Volunteer Gliding School that operated on the weekends flying the Vigilant motor glider. Thus a wide variety of flying was available, further enhanced when the Chipmunks of the Air Experience Flight (AEF) normally based up the road at Leeming deployed to Linton for their summer camp flying.

Needless to say I sampled all types, but not as frequently as I would have liked as there was much to do as Station Commander. Indeed, there was so much going on that it is difficult to single out individual events of note; just a few come to mind in no particular order. There was the changeover at RNEFTS, when a civilian contractor (Hunting) took over the operation with civilian aircraft – the Slingsby Firefly – and a predominantly civilian team of instructors. The Navy put on a tremendous final decommissioning parade and cocktail party but were justifiably enraged to discover that the new contractor had taken down the RNEFTS sign on the hangar and replaced it with its own before the event. The whole experience was a nightmare of non co-operation from the Hunting's manager, which nearly resulted in my Chief Instructor and me resigning; not a happy business at all and what a contrast to what had gone before.

In contrast there was the honour of reading the Lesson in York Minster in the Battle of Britain Service and taking the salute at the Battle of Britain Parade in York, when the Station exercised its Freedom of the City by marching past. Unusually there were German officers taking part in the Parade – they were students on RNEFTS. Then there was the monthly 'Gentleman's Walk' in which a select group of worthies would disappear into the Dales or North York Moors for a day's walking in any weather, always stopping for lunch in one of the numerous excellent Yorkshire pubs.

Despite a distinct lack of long-term funding for the Station we managed to build a large new extension to the Officers' Mess, demolish the dreadful pre-war airmen's married quarters and build some very nice new ones. Eventually the Jet Provosts were retired and had to be flown away to their new homes, but not before we held a big 'Farewell JP' party. Despite horrible weather on the day we managed to put up a big formation in the form of the letters JP, plus a solo aerobatic display. We also managed to get two Piston Provosts to come, plus a large number of those associated with the aircraft during its long RAF service. The day finished with a Happy Hour and Guest Night, with the inevitable headaches the next morning.

Eventually only one JP 3 remained, languishing in the corner of a hangar. I asked the engineers why it was still here – the answer was that the purchaser's cheque had still not been cleared. Eventually the new owner arrived to take his Jet Provost away. He paid for a full fuel load and staggered off the short runway, just missing the trees at the end.

The interesting sequel was that a short time later he had the canopy and right-hand seat removed for some maintenance reason. When the seat was reinstalled the top latch, which secured the seat to the aircraft, was not done up properly. The explosive parts of the ejection seat had been removed but the mechanical parts and parachute were all in working order. He then offered his brother a trip, which was accepted. His brother strapped into the right-hand seat incorrectly, omitting to do up two vital straps. Once airborne he was offered some aerobatics. Again he accepted. During a roll some negative g was experienced and the seat, not properly secured, fell out through the canopy. Its occupant was then released from the seat, which unfortunately remained attached to the parachute. Our hero, with some presence of mind, then pulled the parachute rip cord, opening the parachute. Then the entire parachute and seat combination slid up his body (the straps were not done up) until he was suspended by the neck – luckily for him this occurred so close to the ground that he landed in a heap before he was strangled. The other brother, meanwhile, was aghast when his sibling shot out of the Jet Provost, and, convinced he was dead, took some time to compose himself sufficiently to go back and land. It is interesting to note that at the time of writing (2007) there are still many of our Jet Provosts flying under civilian ownership.

Another interesting little diversion came in the form of a hot air balloon flight. A local balloon operator asked for permission to land at any of our four airfields if they happened to appear conveniently in front of him on one of his flights. I was quite happy to allow him to do so, provided I could see for myself the nature of his activities. Thus an invitation arrived to join one of his flights over the Yorkshire Dales, complete with a champagne reception at the end of the flight. The whole business of inflating the balloon, climbing aboard before it shot off, then drifting in the wind in a wickerwork basket whilst looking vertically down at the scenery and hearing every sound from down below was a new and amazing experience. It was quite unlike flying a conventional aircraft. It was an expensive way of flying but luckily I got my one trip for free.

I recall one unusual incident in the autumn of 1993 when we were staying in our Suffolk house for the weekend. The house is very close to, if not actually on, the extended centre line of runway 29 at the Mildenhall USAF base, about 15 miles away. KC 135 tankers and other heavy US aircraft regularly flew over whilst positioning for an approach. During the night I was woken by a very strange-sounding aircraft passing overhead; the engine noise was a pulsing sound quite unlike anything I'd heard before. I lay in bed, half awake, wondering whether I had dreamt it, when I heard another similar sound approaching. I jumped out of bed and looked out of the window but could see nothing in the pitch black. I ran to the other side of the house and saw a faint flashing light disappearing towards Mildenhall. The time was 02.20 on the Sunday morning.

On return to Linton I related the story to OC Ops Wing, who responded by saying that he knew the senior RAF officer at Mildenhall very well, and that he would ask him what the aircraft were. A few minutes later he rang me to say that Mildenhall had declared that no traffic had recovered there between 1800 hrs on Saturday and 1000 hrs on Sunday. My response was 'Nonsense, two strange aircraft definitely went in early Sunday morning.' OC Ops had another go at Mildenhall, only to be told firmly by his RAF colleague to stop making inquiries at once. So what were they?

At that time there were many rumours of a new stealthy aircraft called Aurora that had been developed to replace the SR71. A few weeks before my experience there had been an unexplained incident at Boscombe Down apparently involving an emergency landing by an unknown US aircraft, after which it was covered in tarpaulins and removed with great secrecy by an American C5 transport aircraft. In the aviation magazines there was great speculation about Aurora, with a few claimed sightings, and descriptions of a pulsing engine noise. By all accounts the project was unsuccessful, as stories soon dried up and no further sightings were recorded. It's my guess that two of these mystery aircraft were recovered into Mildenhall that night, again in great secrecy. I was just lucky enough to be woken up by them.

In April 1994 the Buccaneer was finally retired from service, having been in service with both the RN and the RAF for more than thirty years. A massive weekend party was held at Lossiemouth to say goodbye to this marvellous old warhorse, attended by just about everyone who had ever been involved with the Buccaneer as air or ground crew. One of the outcomes of this weekend was the formation of the Buccaneer Aircrew Association. I found myself nominated as Deputy Chairman and Newsletter Editor. The Association continues to thrive with over 450 members, regular social events including the infamous 'Buccaneer Blitz', held every year in London. The Association even owns its own Buccaneer, rescued from the scrapman's torch and currently displayed in the Yorkshire Air Museum along with many of the weapons used in its operational life.

Eventually, after a six-month extension in post, all good things had to come to an end and it was time to hand over command to another old friend, David Milne- Smith. There was the inevitable round of parties, farewells, presentations and a final Dining Out

Night. At the same time I was frantically negotiating my next tour, which would inevitably be my last in full-time service. After a couple of false starts I ended up with a posting to the MoD in the Defence Exports Services Organisation, my sole posting to the MoD in thirty-seven years of service in the RAF. So it was a sad farewell to Linton and Yorkshire and a move back down to our Suffolk home.

CHAPTER THIRTEEN

MoD, 5 Air Experience Flight and Cambridge University Air Squadron – 1994 to 2010

My first priority was to join No. 5 Air Experience Flight (AEF) at Cambridge Airport, to fly Chipmunks under the redoubtable leadership of Sqn Ldr Ced Hughes. Once this had been achieved I could think about the next tour, which was to be my last as a full-time RAF officer.

However, before this started I suddenly found myself being briefed in the Foreign Office and the MoD on a task that involved travelling to the Gulf state of Qatar, at the request of the Qatari Minister for Defence, to conduct a review of Qatar's defence forces and to make recommendations for the future size and role of these forces. Working with me would be a Royal Navy Captain and an Army Colonel. We only had three weeks to carry out this task due to a lack of funding to pay for a longer stay!

After the withdrawal of the British from the Gulf in the 1970s Qatar had fallen very much under French influence. Most of the Air Force's equipment was French and the ruling elite of Qatar had been actively encouraged by France to remain within the

French sphere of influence. By 1994, however, this relationship was beginning to go sour and the Qataris were now looking to the United Kingdom for advice and assistance. Qatar also had access to potentially one of the largest natural gas fields in the world in its territorial waters.

On arrival we were ushered into the presence of the Minister of State for Defence Affairs, a member of the ruling Al Thani family, who was a rather wild character. He clearly enjoyed extreme sub aqua diving and offered my RN colleague some opportunities, which the Captain tactfully turned down. My task was to deal with the air arm. It was too small really to justify the title of Air Force. It soon became apparent that its leader and his immediate circle were still very much under French influence and resented my appearance in their midst. Getting any help from them was a struggle, whereas my naval colleague had no problems at all, as the head of the Qatari naval arm had been through Dartmouth and was longing for a return to British values! A large number of Pakistanis were also included in the air arm, both as aircrew and engineers. They, too, were deeply suspicious of my activities. Thus I had a particularly difficult three weeks, whereas my naval and army colleagues clearly enjoyed themselves.

Eventually, we presented our findings and recommendations to the Minister and presented him with our only official gift, a rather tacky MoD crest. We, on the other hand, were each given a very expensive watch! We returned to the UK uncertain as to what would be the outcome of our visit. Time was to prove that Qatar moved very positively into the US/UK orbit, with major coalition operations being conducted from there in subsequent years. Our recommendation that a new airfield for sole military use be built was taken up and the Qatari air arm ordered Hawk aircraft to replace its French Alpha Jets, so perhaps we did achieve something.

On my return from Qatar and after a short interlude working at RAF Innsworth, I found myself behind a desk in the Ministry of Defence, working in the Defence Exports Services Organisation as the Assistant Military Deputy (Air), a very grand title for a rather routine job. At least it was possible to escape early on a Friday, take the train to Cambridge and fly the Chipmunk all afternoon or on the weekend. The job did have its compensa-

The 237 OCU Hunter display team pilots, Lossiemouth Air Day, 1986.

The 237 OCU Hunter team in action.

End of sortie and achievement of 2000 hrs Buccaneer flying.

CFS Exam Wing visit to Jordan, 1989. Flying the F5.

CFS Examining Wing, RAF Scampton, 1988. I was current on all aircraft in the photo apart from the Dominie.

Preparing a flarepath of beer cans, Oman. Prior to desert strip night work, 1988.

CFS ExamWing visit, Singapore, 1989. Flying the uncomfortable SF260.

5 Exam Wing visit Dubai, 1989. Flying a micro light.

5 Exam Wing visit Kenya, 1989. Hawks at Mombasa airport.

I had to check out gliding instructors. Gliding at Syerston

CFS, 1989. Flying the Bulldog.

Taking over RAF Linton on Ouse, January 1992.

My staff at Linton.

Flying the Lord Mayor of York, Linton, 1992.

The JP Gate Guardian at Linton, I did my first jet solo in this aircraft, Cranwell, 1962.

IPs on the flight line, Linton, with low fly past from 2 Buccaneers

The Tucano replaced the JP at Linton in 1992.

Flying the Chief Constable of Northumbria, John Stevens, latterly Lord Stevens, Linton, 1993.

hot air balloon trip, 1994. Author far left in the basket.

ne of the Buccaneer Aircrew Association with their Buccaneer, Elvington, 1996. Author 2nd right,
< row.

Tutors of CUAS, RAF Wyton, 2000.

Tutor formation celebrating 100 years of powered flight, 3 Dec 2003.

Tutor formation pilots, 3 Dec 2003. Each one has more than 1000 hrs Tutor flying time.
Author 2nd right, back row.

Flying the Auster at Great Ashfield.

Author at the controls, Auster.

tions in the form of many overseas trips to sort out problems with British products in places such as Korea, Oman and Indonesia, also attending major overseas trade shows and organising tours by the Red Arrows in support of British Industry. The Paris Air Show and Farnborough also featured regularly. Back in London there was a regular involvement with the Air Attaché circuit with its numerous social events. During this tour I had what was to prove to be my last trip in a fast jet during a visit to Valley, although I did not know it at the time.

Time passed quickly and it soon became apparent that the dreaded fifty-fifth birthday was approaching. There was still a need to earn money and retirement from the RAF was about to occur. A job within the aircraft industry was always a possibility but did not really appeal. I scanned the newspapers looking for possibilities and even had a couple of interviews but with no result.

Then, out of the blue, came a totally new and thoroughly appealing possibility. The RAF was going through one of its regular manning crises and was getting short of pilots on the front line. Too many were leaving and the need to remove those remaining from the front line to become flying instructors was making matters worse. The solution was to offer employment to those leaving the Service as Full Time Reservists, on specific contracts at specific locations, as Flight Lieutenant flying instructors. There would be one of these creatures on each University Air Squadron. I was now current again on the Bulldog, as the Chipmunk had now left the AEFs, so I applied for the post of Full Time Reservist QFI on Cambridge University Air Squadron (CUAS), which also flew from Cambridge Airport. This time the interview was successful and I got the job. With great delight I left the MoD as a Group Captain on a Friday, was dined out in great style in the RAF Club, went home and cut my rank tabs in half and went back to work the next Monday as a Flight Lieutenant. The initial contract was for four years.

After a short QFI Refresher course at Cranwell I reported to the oldest University Air Squadron in the world at Cambridge Airport to be plunged immediately into the mad house of Freshers' Fair where our new recruits were to be found. For two years the squadron remained at Cambridge Airport, an ideal location for the majority of our students, as it was only a short cycle ride from the University area. It was also only a forty-minute drive for me from home.

In 1999 the squadron won the de Havilland Trophy in the regional competition but already the signs of a major change were on the horizon. A decision to replace the Bulldog had finally been made; the new aircraft was to be the Grob 115E, named Tutor, supplied and serviced by a civil contractor. The aircraft was owned by the contractor, not the MoD, and would be civil registered. This meant restrictions on many traditional flying activities, such as low flying below 500 feet. The squadron was also required to move from Cambridge Airport to RAF Wyton, an airfield that had been closed since 1995, which was to be reactivated as the base airfield for Cambridge University Air Squadron and University of London Air Squadron. It was some 15 miles away from Cambridge, in the wrong direction for me, and quite a challenge for students without cars to get to.

We were the first squadron to be re-equipped with the Tutor, an event that was coincident with the move to Wyton. The 'new' accommodation at Wyton had been lying derelict for four years, there was no running water, no lavatories, the windows were frosted over so you could not see out and the CAA refused to license the hangar for use as it had no heating. It was clearly going to be a struggle to get the place sorted out. The airfield was, however, ideal for light aircraft operations, surrounded by open countryside (unlike Cambridge) with good access to un-restricted airspace. It took just over two years to get everything finished, including new mini hangars inside the main hangar for aircraft servicing, a decent-sized aircraft parking area, adequate Air Traffic Control and reactivation of the secondary runway.

The Tutor was a very different type of trainer when compared with the Bulldog. It was built of carbon fibre and had a very extensive avionics fit, including an embedded Global Positioning System (GPS) that would even allow instrument approaches to be flown without any external equipment apart from a small radio box in the Air Traffic Control Tower. It handled very benignly apart from in cross-wind landings, the main landing gear having no form of damping. After some eighteen months of operations it was discovered that the aircraft was not certified to fly in cloud. A long and difficult period followed whilst this problem was resolved; after modification the restriction was lifted, only to be replaced by another that prevented many traditional aerobatic manoeuvres being flown because they had not been specifically cleared for the aircraft.

All told, it was a frustrating period but it didn't seem to upset the students very much. Life on the squadron generally carried on much as before, with plenty of sailing and skiing expeditions and many social activities in the wonderful Town Headquarters in Cambridge. A wide variety of students came through the squadron. Quite a few opted for a career in the RAF as a result of their experience, whilst others disappeared into civilian life with a small taste of military flying, but they all enjoyed their time on CUAS.

For most of my time on CUAS I was the CFI, which involved arranging the daily term-time flying programmes, running the vacation flying camps and organising the annual summer camp away at some other airfield. We went to Coltishall twice, Woodvale and St Athan until our Headquarters at Cranwell decided that University Air Squadrons didn't need to go away for the summer any more, probably because they realised that we were having too much fun when away from home base.

I also renewed my Instrument Rating Examiner qualification, was responsible for squadron history (including organising the 75th Anniversary celebrations) and was the Squadron Adventurous Training Officer. It was a busy time but most enjoyable, apart from the 60-mile each-way commute every day. I eventually got rid of the CFI task, only to be made Chief Ground Instructor. The title seemed to indicate that there were other ground instructors, but no, I was the only one. This involved organising all the ground training activities, as well as continuing to fly full time.

December 2003 marked the 100th anniversary of the first powered controlled flight, so the two UAS at Wyton put up a formation of five Tutors to mark this auspicious occasion. The aircraft were flown entirely by full-time reservist QFIs, all of whom had over 1000 hours' flying time on the Tutor, and whose combined total of flying hours and years of RAF service amounted to 34,000 hours and 190 years. Two of us, Syd Morris and I, had flown together in a fifty-five aircraft formation over Aden thirty-six years previously. During my time on CUAS I was presented with a small memento to mark my forty years as a qualified military pilot, something not many aviators can claim to have achieved.

During my time with CUAS a slightly spooky event occurred at home. In 1940 my father commanded 263 Squadron from June to December. It was the first squadron to be equipped with the Westland Whirlwind, the RAF's first single-seat, twin-engine fighter. In the 1980s Air Vice-Marshal Ken Hayr, who had been a Flight Cadet when my father was Commandant at Cranwell in the 1950s, was Air Officer Commanding No. 11 Group, the only fighter group in the RAF at that time. Ken Hayr used to invite small groups of veterans from the Fighter Command of the 1940s to his Headquarters for an informal lunch, after which each veteran would be presented with a model of the aircraft he flew in 1940. My father was invited to one of these lunch parties, and Ken Hayr duly presented him with a lovely model of a Whirlwind, which I subsequently inherited when my father died in 1992.

The Whirlwind model lived in my study, on a bookshelf about two and a half feet above floor level. Meanwhile Ken Hayr retired from the RAF and became a display pilot on the air show circuit, flying a variety of aircraft. In particular, he displayed a Vampire T11 trainer. During the Biggin Hill Air Show of 2002 Ken was tragically killed when he lost control of the Vampire he was flying when he encountered powerful jet wake from the Sea Vixen ahead of him at too low an altitude to eject. The next morning I found the shattered remains of the Whirlwind model in the garden; our golden retriever dog, just over a year old, had removed it from the shelf, taken it outside and chewed it to bits. There were a number of other models he could easily have chosen, but it was the one given by Ken Hayr to my father. The dog has never touched another model again despite there being many within reach. It was really quite a strange affair.

Another element of aviation came into my life at this time when I was asked to join a volunteer team of pilots who formed the Flying Control Committee at the Imperial War Museum, Duxford. We were all highly experienced military aviators with some display flying background. Our role was to ensure that the rules governing display flying were adhered to during displays at Duxford, to advise and assist the organisers and to ensure that those who broke the rules or who flew dangerously were dealt with appropriately. This was a sensitive and sometimes difficult task as those who flew varied enormously in skill levels and in their attitude to discipline in the air. It required a delicate and diplomatic touch. The bonus was the privilege of mixing with many pilots flying unique and exotic aircraft, most dating from the 1940s to 1950s, and having a free ringside seat at all Duxford's superb air displays.

Unfortunately, when something goes badly wrong there is usually insufficient time to do anything about it. During the 'Flying Legends' Display of 2003 the RN Historic Flight Firefly was being flown by a relatively inexperienced pilot. This was the very same aircraft that we had brought back to the UK in HMS *Victorious* way back in the summer of 1967, so I had a particular interest in it. The aircraft was being flown downwind, just outside the airfield boundary, to reposition for its next pass. I was watching it from the roof of the Control Tower. It pulled up into a Derry wing-over and immediately flicked into a spin, which was clearly irrecoverable from such a low height. Clearly the pilot had entered the manoeuvre with insufficient energy and it was all over in seconds. The aircraft crashed into a field of wheat, just missing houses in Duxford village, instantly killing both crew in full view of the capacity crowd. There was nothing any of us could have done. However, had we been made aware of the pilot's lack of display experience we might have been able to make him remove that manoeuvre from his display routine, but unfortunately we had not been given his display sequence. After this tragedy the Committee was given access to all display sequences before flying started. So far, there have been no further accidents and I hope it stays that way.

It became clear in 2004 that contracts for Full Time Reservists were not going to be renewed when they expired. Thus for me the end of full-time military aviation became a reality. I was dined out of the squadron in great style in November 2004 after forty-four years of full-time service in the RAF and over 8000 hours of flying in twenty-eight different military aircraft types. However, this was not quite the end of the story. I joined No. 5 Air Experience Flight in the lowly rank of Flying Officer RAF Volunteer Reserve (Training), to fly members of the Air Training Corps and Combined Cadet Force on air experience trips. This involves a trip to RAF Wyton once a week, to fly the Tutor on short twenty-minute sorties. It is very enjoyable and a delightful way to wind down slowly to the time when ultimately I shall have to hand in my flying suit and helmet for the last time. Sometimes the cadets ask me how long I have been flying as a pilot. When I respond with 'more than forty years' they are usually stunned into silence, such a long time being inconceivable to a twenty-first century teenager. I just hope some of them will have the luck to have as much fun as I have had.

Eventually all good things come to an end. In 2010 it was decided by higher authority that those pilots aged over 65 could no longer be trusted to fly Air Cadets due to risk of them becoming incapacitated in the air, despite their regular medical checks. I handed in my flying helmet after some 50 years in the cockpit and exactly 8500 flying hours in the RAF, a neat figure to sign off with. I stillmaintain close contact with aviation as a Liveryman of the Honourable Comapany of Air Pilots, editing its bi-monthly journey 'Air-Pilot', and continuing to serve on the Flying Control Committee at Duxford. The passion for flying has not yet been extinguished!

CHAPTER FOURTEEN

The Good, the Bad and the Ugly

S o, after more than fifty years and over 8500 hours of military flying, in a wide range of very different types, which was the best, the most effective, the easiest, the most difficult, the strangest, the worst and the least memorable?

Two of the best for me were the Chipmunk and the Hunter F6. At opposite ends of the performance spectrum, they both were very good to look at, particularly the Hunter. Both had beautifully responsive and well balanced handling qualities, they were easy to fly but demanding to fly well. Both had cockpits with a distinctive smell and neither was particularly comfortable, but sortie lengths in each were usually quite short. The Chipmunk could be very tricky in a cross wind and the Hunter could bite if you exceeded 0.85 M with any flap selected. The Hunter could also use up fuel very quickly. In spite of the countless forced landings practised in each, neither ever gave me the slightest hint of an unserviceable engine. Both were absolute classics from the best manufacturers of British aircraft, Hawkers and de Havilland.

The most effective was without doubt the Buccaneer. It had enormous character and some very quirky handling characteristics but was perfect for the role for which it was designed – low-level strike, attack and reconnaissance. Throughout its service life it was regularly modified to carry a wide range of weapons, although most regrettably the avionics hardly changed from the day it entered service with the RN. The list of weapons it was able to deliver is amazing: the 'Red Beard' tactical nuclear weapon; the WE 177 nuclear weapon; 1000-lb and 540-lb bombs; 2-inch RP, Gloworm RP; SNEB RP; Lepus flares; Bullpup ASM; MARTEL TV and AR ASM; Sea Eagle ASM; Sidewinder AIM 9B, 9G and 9L; laser-guided 1000-lb bombs; and numerous types of practice bomb. From 1978 until 1991 it was the only RAF aircraft able to provide laser designation for laser-guided bombs with video recording. It performed outstandingly well in both the maritime and overland theatres, based both at sea and ashore. In the twilight of its service it flew with great effectiveness in the first Gulf war, designating and delivering laser-guided bombs from high level, a role that had never been envisaged on its entry into service in the 1960s.

The easiest to fly was the Jet Provost 3. Its handling characteristics were extremely docile and it was virtually unbreakable. The Viper engine gave it only a modest performance, which allowed the tyro pilot plenty of time to cope with his new and unfamiliar environment. In many ways it was perhaps too easy to fly, generating a false sense of confidence, which rapidly evaporated when confronted with an aircraft with a more robust performance. The Jet Provost 3 was often referred to as 'the constant thrust, variable noise machine', an apt epithet.

The most difficult aircraft I ever had the pleasure of flying was without doubt the Shackleton AEW2. It was huge and ungainly to manoeuvre on the ground, its tail wheel configuration making it basically unstable. Excessive use of the pneumatically operated brakes resulted in a loss of pneumatic pressure, which then required a lengthy recharging process. In the air it was heavy and slow to respond to control inputs, requiring much anticipation. Landing was always very challenging, particularly in a cross wind. Anything other than a perfect three-point touchdown would result in a series of kangaroo-like bounces that became increasingly difficult to control. It was very noisy inside and has doubtless deafened many aircrew who flew it for lengthy periods. Flying the Shackleton filled me with admiration for those young men who flew Lancasters during World War Two, as single pilots with relatively few flying hours, on long, hazardous bombing missions over Germany at night. I suspect that the Hastings would fall into the same category as the

Shackleton, but as all I ever did was to raise and lower the landing gear, I am not qualified to comment further!

The prize for the strangest goes to the Short Skyvan, flown in the Oman. It looked like a freight container that had wings bolted on, together with some wheels to facilitate movement on the ground. It was, nevertheless, ideal for flying all sorts of unusual people, animals and freight around the harsh environment of the Oman. It was robust, simple and straightforward to fly.

As for the worst, for me it was the Jetstream T1. Designed by the famous firm of Handley Page as a small commuter airliner, it was intended to fly between regional airports at a constant speed and height, and this it did very well. It was never suited to the role of pilot training, with the constant take-offs and landings, the regular explorations of the flight envelope at medium and low levels and the general hard wear and tear of training flying. The engines were far too complex, controlled by a myriad of micro-switches. It was difficult to land and very noisy inside. The view from the flight deck, whilst adequate for take-off, transit along an airway and landing, was not really good enough for lookout in a busy circuit or during general handling. It was far from ideal as a multi-engine pilot training aircraft. However, it fulfilled this role from the late 1970s until 2003 without loss, other than its pilots' hearing. Since the formation of the RAF in 1918 there had always been a Handley Page aircraft in RAF service, until 2003, when the Jetstream was finally retired, although some soldier on with the RN as crew trainers.

The least memorable candidate comes from the motley collection of civil aircraft I have been able to fly over the last forty odd years. It is the Premier AX3 microlight, a device I had a couple of trips in whilst serving at RAF Brampton as Group Captain Flying Training. We were looking into the possibility of using microlights to provide air experience for Air Cadets and the Premier AX3 was offered for trial as a potential vehicle for this. It was flimsy, very underpowered and generally uninspiring. I flew in it from Wyton to Scampton and back again but it would have been quicker to have gone by car.

Record of Service

Sep 1960 to Jul 1963	RAF College Cranwell (officer and flying training)
Aug 1963 to Feb 1964	4 FTS RAF Valley (flying training)
Feb 1964 to Apr 1964	36 Squadron RAF Colerne (holding post)
Apr 1964 to Jul 1964	231 OCU RAF Bassingbourn (operational conversion)
Aug 1964 to Jul 1966	16 Squadron RAF Laarbruch (squadron pilot)
Jul 1966 to Nov 1966	736 NAS RNAS Lossiemouth (operational conversion)
Dec 1966 to Jul 1968	801 NAS HMS *Victorious*/RNAS Lossiemouth (squadron pilot)
Aug 1968 to Dec 1968	244 QFI Course RAF Little Rissington (flying instructor course)
Jan 1969 to May 1969	4 FTS RAF Valley (flying instructor)
Jun 1969 to Mar 1971	736 NAS RNAS Lossiemouth (flying instructor)
Apr 1971 to Jun 1972	237 OCU RAF Honington (flying instructor)

Jul 1972 to Mar 1975	12 Squadron RAF Honington (squadron pilot and training officer)
Apr 1975 to Sep 1977	79 Squadron RAF Brawdy (Flight Commander and flying instructor)
Sep 1977 to Dec 1979	237 OCU RAF Honington (Chief Flying Instructor)
Jan 1980 to Dec 1980	RAF Staff College Bracknell (student)
Jan 1981 to Oct 1982	RAF Strike Command, High Wycombe (Personal Staff Officer to Deputy C-in-C)
Oct 1982 to Mar 1984	RAF Support Command, Brampton (air staff officer)
Apr 1984 to Jun 1987	237 OCU RAF Honington, RAF Lossiemouth (Officer Commanding)
Jul 1987 to Dec 1989	CFS RAF Scampton (Officer Commanding CFS Examining Wing)
Jan 1990 to Dec 1991	RAF Support Command, Brampton (Group Captain Flying Training)
Jan 1992 to Jul 1994	RAF Linton-on-Ouse (Station Commander)
Aug 1994 to Feb 1995	RAF Personnel and Training Command, Innsworth (Project Officer, future flying training)
Mar 1995 to Sep 1997	MoD, DESO (Assistant Military Deputy, Air)
Sep1997 to Nov 2004	Cambridge University Air Squadron, Cambridge Airport and RAF Wyton (Chief Flying Instructor, Chief Ground Instructor)
Dec 2004 to Sep 2010	5 AEF RAF Wyton (pilot)

Pilot Qualifications, Military Aircraft

JET

FIRST PILOT, DAY/NIGHT

Jet Provost T3, 3A, 4, 5A
Gnat T1
Canberra B 2, T4, B(I)8
Hunter F6, F(GA) 9, GA 11,T7, 7A, 8, 8B, 8C
Buccaneer S1, 2
Hawk T1, 61

FIRST PILOT DAY

Phantom FGR 2
F5F
S 211
Macchi MB 326, 329

TURBO PROP

FIRST PILOT DAY/NIGHT

Jetstream T1

Skyvan
Tucano T 1

FIRST PILOT DAY

Jetstream T3

PISTON

FIRST PILOT DAY/NIGHT

Bulldog T1
Shackleton AEW 2

FIRST PILOT DAY

Chipmunk T 10
SF 260 Warrior
Firefly T 67 M
G 115 E Tutor
Defender

SECOND PILOT

Hastings C 1, 2

GLIDERS

FIRST PILOT DAY

Venture T1
Viking T1
Valiant ASW 19
Vanguard T1
Vigilant T1

HELICOPTER

FIRST PILOT DAY

Gazelle HT 3

ANNEX 3

Flying Hours

Buccaneer	2185
Hunter	1416
Canberra	600
JP	400
Hawk	323
Gnat	195
Tucano	226
Jetstream	110
Tutor	1652
Bulldog	752
Chipmunk	135
Multi-engine piston, rotary, glider and miscellaneous types	508

ANNEX 4

Civilian Aircraft Flown as First Pilot

Auster

RV 8

Robin

Cessna 150

Hornet Moth

Luton Minor

CFM Shadow

Fournier RF3

Andreasson B4

Premier AX3

Luscombe Silvaire

Boeing Stearman

Flying the Buccaneer, a Pilot's Perspective

Written for the Japanese magazine *Famous Airplanes of the World* and reproduced with its permission.

I first became involved with the Buccaneer in July 1966, when I arrived at the Royal Naval Air Station Lossiemouth in the north of Scotland, to embark on an exchange tour of duty as an RAF pilot with the Fleet Air Arm of the Royal Navy. After two years of flying with 801 Naval Air Squadron embarked on the aircraft carriers HMS *Victorious* and *Hermes*, I became a flying instructor and returned to serve on the operational training unit, 736 Naval Air Squadron. This involved the somewhat alarming business of flying in the observer's seat, with no flying controls, to assist a pilot on his first ever flight in a Buccaneer. By 1971 the Buccaneer had been brought into service with the Royal Air Force and I spent another year on 237 Operational Conversion Unit, the RAF Buccaneer training squadron, as an instructor. I then spent three years on 12 Squadron, the first RAF Buccaneer squadron, as the training officer and squadron pilot. During this time many new weapons and tactics were introduced, including the Martel air to surface missile system. I was awarded the Queen's Commendation for Valuable Services in the Air at the end of this assignment. In 1977 I returned to 237 Operational Conversion Unit as a Flight Commander and Chief Flying Instructor, again teaching the art of flying the Buccaneer. After this assignment I remained on ground duties until 1984, when I returned to command 237

Operational Conversion Unit, moving it from its base in the east of England back to Lossiemouth in Scotland. I relinquished command in 1987. Overall I was associated with the Buccaneer for 21 years and flew over 2000 hrs in the aircraft. I also flew over 1000 hrs in the dual control Hawker Hunter, which was used as a trainer for the Buccaneer.

The first version of the Buccaneer, the S1, was powered by de Havilland Gyron Junior turbo jets, each gave a static thrust of 7100 lb, barely adequate for such a large and heavy aircraft. By mid 1966 the S1 version was being steadily replaced in service by the S2, which was powered by Rolls-Royce Spey turbo fans, rated to give 11,500 lb of thrust. I learnt to fly on the S1 before moving on to the S2, which was used by the operational squadrons.

Before flying the Buccaneer at least two weeks were spent in the Ground Training School, learning how the aircraft's complex systems worked. Considerable time was also spent in the Flight Simulator. The first Simulator was fairly rudimentary, with no motion or visual capability, but it did allow the pilot and his observer/navigator to practise normal and emergency procedures in a fairly realistic environment. Later Simulators for the S2 version had more sophisticated facilities including motion, a visual system and the ability to carry out weapon attack profiles. There was no dual control facility in the Buccaneer, so a number of Hawker Hunter trainers, equipped with the Buccaneer flight instrument system, were used to introduce trainee pilots to the flying techniques used in the Buccaneer, although in no way did they replicate the Buccaneer's flying characteristics.

The first thing you noticed as you walked out to a Buccaneer was its size – it was a big aircraft, weighing in at around 20 tons, 64 feet long and with a wingspan of 44 feet. It was quite a climb up into the cockpit, which was fitted with Martin-Baker Mk6 MSB ejection seats. Early Naval aircraft had an underwater ejection system fitted to the seat; this used compressed air to release the occupant's harness, inflate his lifejacket and propel him to the surface if the aircraft landed in the sea with the aircrew still in it. It was initiated by a water depth sensor. The introduction of a rocket pack to the seat in 1970 gave it a 'zero/zero' capability so the underwater escape facility was no longer needed. Cockpit instrumentation was somewhat haphazard. The excellent OR946 Integrated Flight Instrument

System (IFIS), driven by a Master Reference Gyro and an Air Data Computer, was rather overshadowed by the proliferation of other random instruments; these seemed to increase every time a modification was embodied. For example, the IFIS airspeed display, a strip indication, was not considered accurate enough or suitably positioned for speed assessment during carrier operations, so a two-needle conventional airspeed indicator was fitted on the top of the left instrument panel to give the pilot an accurate 'heads up' airspeed display. By the end of the aircraft's life the cockpit could best be described as an ergonomic slum. In front of the pilot was the Strike Sight, a simple head up display, which used a sight glass that could be folded down to improve forward visibility. The aircraft also had a very effective windscreen clearance hot air jet and a wiper/washer (just like your car), both essential for operations over the sea. The Buccaneer had a complex flying control system. In addition to conventional ailerons, flaps, rudder and all moving tailplane, there were two innovative high lift devices that enabled the Buccaneer to be launched from and landed back on the rather small Royal Navy aircraft carriers. The ailerons could be drooped to a maximum of 25 degrees, to act as additional flaps. This produced a very strong nose down change of trim, which was counteracted by an electrically operated flap on the rear of the tailplane that moved upwards through the same amount as the ailerons drooped, thus restoring longitudinal control. A boundary layer control system ejected high pressure air, bled from the engines, over the wing leading edge, the top surfaces of the flaps and ailerons and the under surface of the tailplane. The combination of aileron droop, tailplane flap and the boundary layer control system (BLC) reduced the minimum speed achievable from 155 kts to 130 kts, thus enabling catapult launch and arrested landings on aircraft carriers.

The twin Speys, or Gyron Juniors in a Mk1, were started by using an external low pressure air starter, there being no onboard starter system, something to be borne in mind when operating away from home base. Once the engines were running and the various systems had been checked, taxiing was straightforward, there being ample power and authority from the brakes and nose wheel steering. The facility to fold the wings was very useful when manoeuvring in confined spaces, and allowed more than one aircraft to be positioned within a Hardened Aircraft Shelter.

Catapult launch from a carrier was carried out with hands off the control column. A tailplane angle was calculated and set so that the aircraft would rotate a small amount on leaving the deck; mainplane flap/aileron droop/tailplane flap was set to its maximum deflection of 45/25/25 with the Boundary Layer Control (BLC) system on. The aircraft was physically connected to the carrier deck by a frangible metal link known as the 'hold back'. This would prevent the aircraft from moving with full power applied but would break when the catapult was fired, thereby releasing the aircraft and allowing it to accelerate under the thrust of the catapult. After the hold back had been connected, the catapult bridle was attached and the catapult shuttle was moved forwards, thereby rotating the aircraft into the nose up launch attitude. Once 'tensioned up' in the launch attitude full power was applied under the direction of the Flight Deck Officer. When ready to launch the pilot would brace his left arm to ensure full power remained applied, raise his right hand to indicate he was ready to go to the Flight Deck Officer, then place his hand on his right thigh adjacent to, but not holding, the control column. Acceleration down the catapult was very brisk – about 4 to 5 g – and once airborne the pilot would take control whilst being careful not to induce a high pitch rate, as the Buccaneer was unstable in pitch at low speed. After retracting the landing gear and cleaning up the flap and droop in stages, the S2 accelerated quickly to its normal operating speed of 420–480 kts, whilst the S1 took considerably longer.

Take-offs from runways were carried out unblown with flap/droop set to 15/10/10, unless aircraft weight or runway length required a blown take-off, when flap/droop was set to 30/20/20. The Buccaneer S1 was slow to accelerate, even when unblown, and needed a long runway, but the Buccaneer S2 accelerated quickly and had a much shorter take-off run. Take-offs in close formation presented no difficulty.

Once airborne, both versions of the Buccaneer were a delight to handle when in their element of high speed at low level, however, the S1 was rather underpowered. Control forces were well balanced and light. The S1's rate of climb was poor, but the S2 gained altitude very quickly. It was unusual to go above

35,000 feet in either version but 40,000 feet could be reached in a light aircraft. The maximum permitted speed was 580 kts or 0.95 M, which could be maintained for ages and easily exceeded. Because of the need to fit the Buccaneer inside the limited head-room of aircraft carrier hangar decks the fin was relatively short, so the aircraft was unstable in yaw, particularly at high speeds. A three axis auto stabilisation system, with a standby yaw damper, was used at all times. There was also an autopilot facility that provided airspeed, heading and height holds, a useful facility on long transit flights. Aerobatic manoeuvres such as aileron rolls, barrel rolls and roll off the top of loops were permitted but full loops were not. The aircraft could suffer from inertia coupling if certain handling limitations were ignored. The Gyron Junior turbo jets in the S1 were very prone to compressor stall, particularly at high angles of attack, so required careful handling. Loss of engine thrust in a Buccaneer S1 was major emergency, particularly in the high drag landing configuration, as the aircraft had a very limited performance on one engine. The Spey turbo fans in the Buccaneer S2 were much more reliable. Single engine flight in the S2 presented no problems.

The Buccaneer could carry a wide range of conventional weapons and could also deliver a tactical nuclear bomb. At first this was a weapon named Red Beard; it was a large device that completely filled the bomb bay and it could only be delivered from a toss manoeuvre. It was replaced in 1971 by a smaller weapon, the WE177; two of these could be carried and they could be delivered from a low level approach in a laydown mode in addition to a toss attack. High explosive and nuclear bombs could be delivered from toss attacks initiated from a high speed, low level approach. The observer/navigator would use his radar to identify and lock on to a target. The pilot would follow the steering demands displayed in his Strike Sight, pulling up into a 3–4 g toss profile about 3 miles from the target. Dive bombing and level attacks were also possible with high explosive bombs and rocket projectiles. The Buccaneer also carried a number of different air to surface missiles, such as Bullpup, TV and AR Martel and Sea Eagle, and for self defence a Sidewinder air to air missile, at first the AIM9B but later this was superseded by the AIM9G and 9L. Toss attack profiles were initiated at 540 kts, dive and level attack profiles were flown in the 450–500 kt range. The very wide range of weapons available made for challenging and exciting flying; the Buccaneer was an excellent weapons platform, being stable and responsive in the speed range of 350–550 kts. The rotating weapons door could be opened at speeds up to 550 kts and did not affect aircraft handling in any way.

Both versions of the Buccaneer were equipped for air to air refuelling through a fixed probe, slightly offset to the right in front of the pilot. The first Buccaneer S1s had a retractable probe but this never proved to be satisfactory. Air to air refuelling was carried out at the relatively slow speed of 250–280 kts. The Buccaneer could carry a Flight Refuelling Mk.20 air to air re-fuelling pod under the right wing and this facility was regularly used by the RN squadrons. The RAF squadrons tended to use Victor and VC10 tanker aircraft and only limited use was made of the Buccaneer's pod. The probe was well positioned and re-fuelling in flight fairly straightforward provided there was no turbulence. The technique used was to position the aircraft about 10 metres behind the hose and then to fly steadily towards the basket up the extended line of the hose with an overtaking speed of about 5 kts, adding just a little power as the probe engaged the basket to ensure a positive contact. Once in contact it was necessary to push the hose further into the pod to initiate fuel flow. When refuelling was completed the aircraft would withdraw slowly down the line of the hose until the basket disengaged from the probe. It was important not to look at, but through, the basket during approach and withdrawal in order to reduce the tendency to over control in pitch and generate a pilot induced oscillation.

When speed was reduced below 300 kts for recovery the Buccaneer became much more difficult to fly accurately. There was an aileron gear change facility that allowed greater aileron deflection for the amount of control column movement which could be used below 300 kts. Approaches to both airfields and aircraft carriers were normally flown in the 45/25/25 BLC on configuration, airbrake fully extended, with the final approach being flown at a constant speed for a no flare landing. With 25 degrees of aileron droop extended there was significant adverse aileron yaw generated in turns by the down going aileron but this could be easily resolved by a coordinated use of the rudder. The excellent Airstream Direction Detector (ADD) gave both audio and visual indication of angle of attack/airspeed, allowing the pilot to keep his eyesight out of the cockpit – essential for accurate deck landings. The basic final approach speed (blown) was 127 kts, considerably lower than similar fast jets. It increased to 155 kts unblown. Single engine approaches could be flown either blown at 30/20/20 – essential if landing on a carrier – or unblown at 45/10/10, the usual option for an airfield landing. There was no asymmetric handling problem and the S2 could overshoot on one engine from the threshold providing the fuel state was reduced to a minimum. Single engine touch and go landings in the configuration 30/20/20 BLC on were regularly practised by pilots prior to embarkation to cater for missing a wire on a single engine approach to the carrier. Arrested landings afloat involved a very rapid deceleration; once stopped it was essential to raise the hook, fold the wings and vacate the flight deck quickly to enable subsequent aircraft to land without delay. On airfields arrested landings were carried out in the event of aircraft hydraulic failures; these were straightforward and gave a much slower deceleration. Aborted take-offs could also use the airfield arrestor system to bring the aircraft to a halt.

As previously mentioned, there was no dual control version of the Buccaneer so a pilot's first flight was always a rather stressful event. Another pilot instructor would accompany him in the observer's seat, giving verbal instructions and encouragement but without any chance of taking over control if the student pilot made serious errors. This system worked effectively and I carried out many first flights from the observer's seat without incident as an instructor until one day when I was with a young pilot in a Buccaneer S1. On his first approach to the runway he allowed the aircraft to get too high and so I instructed him to overshoot and try again. As he applied full power the left engine failed. With only one engine working the aircraft would not maintain height and speed, so at an altitude of about 150 feet and at a very low speed I ordered an ejection, I pulled the lower handle of the seat and was fired out of the aircraft. The student pilot followed shortly afterwards and we both landed safely on the airfield. I unfortunately damaged my back badly. The Buccaneer crashed on the airfield and caught fire, giving the airfield rescue services a wonderful opportunity to exercise their skills for real.

In conclusion, the Buccaneer was a challenging aircraft to fly, with its complex systems and its unique and innovative high lift devices and flying controls. All those lucky enough to fly it were highly enthusiastic about it. After 8000 hrs of military flying on many different types I still feel that my 2185 hrs on the Buccaneer, both at sea and shore based, with the Royal Navy and the Royal Air Force, were the most demanding and exciting of my flying career.

Acronyms

AAM	Air to Air Missile
AAR	Air to Air Refuelling
ACRB	Aircrew Refreshment Buffet
ADD	Airstream Direction Detector
ADIZ	Air Defence Identification Zone
AEF	Air Experience Flight
ASM	Air to Surface Missile
ATA	Air Turbine Alternator
BLC	Boundary Layer Control
CFI	Chief Flying Instructor
CFS	Central Flying School
DLP	Deck Landing Practice
FDO	Flight Deck Officer
FRA	First Run Attack
HDU	Head Up Display
IFIS	Integrated Flight Instrument System
IGV	Inlet Guide Vane
IRI	Instrument Rating Instructor
ILS	Instrument Landing System
LABS	Low Altitude Bombing System
LGB	Laser Guided Bomb
MADDL	Mirror Assisted Dummy Deck Landing
NAS	Naval Air Squadron
OCU	Operational Conversion Unit
PSO	Personal Staff Officer

QFI	Qualified Flying Instructor
QRA	Quick Reaction Alert
RNAS	Royal Naval Air Station
RNEFTS	Royal Navy Elementary Flying Training Squadron
RP	Rocket Projectile
RPM	Revolutions Per Minute
TACAN	Tactical Air Navigation Aid
TCV	Turbine Cooling Valve
TWU	Tactical Weapons Unit
UAS	University Air Squadron

Index